THE ACCUSED

THE DREYFUS TRILOGY

Je n'ai qu'une passion, celle de la lumière au nom de l'humanité qui a tant souffert et qui a droit au bonheur. Ma protestation enflammée n'est que le cri de mon âme. Qu'on ose donc me traduire en cours d'assise et que l'enquête ait lieu au grand jour !

J'attends.

GEORGE R. WHYTE

THE ACCUSED

THE
DREYFUS
TRILOGY

INTER NATIONES

Cover illustration
"J'accuse" Scene from the Berlin performance of the opera
Dreyfus – Die Affäre with Artur Korn as Emile Zola

Frontispice
Emile Zola, *J'accuse*, Facsimile text of the last paragraph

Head of editorial board
Georg Blochmann

Editorial board
Andreas Hinz, Sarah Nathan-Davis, Renate Vollmer

Design
Jochen Flörchinger, Jochen Fritz, Andreas Hinz

Production, typesetting, lithography
sec GmbH, Osnabrück, Germany

Printing and binding
sdv Saarbrücker Druckerei und Verlag GmbH,
Saarbrücken, Germany

**A limited and numbered edition
of 100 additional copies has been produced.**

ISBN of the edition by SECOLO publishing house,
Osnabrück, Germany: 3-929979-28-4

TABLE OF CONTENTS

PREFACE

INTER NATIONES, a German media institution devoted to the cultural dialogue between Germany and other countries, is always aware of issues of importance in European and World affairs. The reader of this book may perhaps ask whether an artistic reappraisal of the Dreyfus Affair fits into this framework and why INTER NATIONES has supported a television film on the subject.

In my view there is no doubt that the Dreyfus Affair was a clear expression of anti-Semitism which reached its terrible culmination in the Shoah under the Third Reich. This establishes its link with Germany and our sense of grief. It is also a signal for us to impede through intensive cultural dialogue the persecution of religious or ethnic minorities anywhere in the world.

We will be happy if INTER NATIONES can make a small contribution to that end with this publication. We are also happy to bring George Whyte's excellent research work and artistic adaptation of the Affair to still further international recognition. All this will not remain undiscussed but that will do no harm. Without debate, cultural dialogue would die and without cultural dialogue, there can be no international understanding.

I wish our readers an interesting encounter with an explosive subject. INTER NATIONES would be very glad to receive readers' reactions.

Bonn, March 1996

Dr. Dieter W. Benecke
Chairman INTER NATIONES

TUA RES AGITUR

BARTHOLD C. WITTE

In 1933, when Adolf Hitler had just taken power in Germany, Thomas Mann, the world famous German author, having read a newly published book about the Dreyfus Affair, made the following comment:

"Tua Res Agitur. By Tua Res I mean: This is also the cause of your nation, your country, your own conscience."

Indeed, this was the cause in Germany, in 1933, at the beginning of the Third Reich and thus of the road which led to the Shoah. Is it still the cause for the living generations, more than sixty years later?

George R. Whyte, the author of the *Dreyfus Trilogy*, is convinced that anti-Semitism with all its deadly consequences not only can happen again, but is already happening. My daily newspaper unfortunately shows how right he is, not only with regard to my country but also to the rest of the world. Fortunately it also gives ample reasons for hope. The battle between right and wrong goes on and will certainly never end. But the troops fighting for human dignity, personal freedom and tolerance are at present stronger than the forces of hatred, racism and anti-Semitism. This is true also for Germany, where some time ago citizens went to the streets by the millions, demonstrating against racist hatred and for peaceful understanding. After all, the great majority of Germans learnt the lesson to be drawn from the horrible past and the German role in it.

So why remember the Dreyfus Affair? Has it still something to say, a century later? True, it caught in its time (1894 to 1906) the awesome attention of the whole world. But that happened under political and social conditions which differ greatly from those in our time. Is it possible at all, and particularly in this case, to revive history and draw conclusions for the present? Hannah Arendt, the great political philosopher, who like Th. Mann emigrated from Germany, gives a convincing answer. "The Dreyfus Affair", she says in her famous book about totalitarian rule, "is the culmination of the anti-Semitism which grew out of the special conditions of the nation state but in its violent form foreshadowed future developments ... The main actors of the Affair sometimes seemed to be staging a huge dress rehearsal for a performance put off for more than three decades", that is until 1933.

When looking at how the Affair developed step by step, it is not difficult to follow Arendt's line of interpretation. At its beginning, however, the drama seemed to be rather inconspicuous. Alfred Dreyfus was neither a hero nor a great actor on scene. He just happened to be the first Jew ever who was permitted to join the French General Staff and the French Intelligence. A ranking captain, thirty-five years old, happily married with two children, with a bourgeois family background – if he had not been a Jew his name would never have appeared in the history books, at least during peace time. Suddenly he is pushed into the limelight under the accusation of treason by espionage in favour of the enemy, that is Germany. Already his first trial ending in December 1894 with conviction to lifelong imprisonment, deportation to Devil's Island and degradation bears all the elements of a scandal.

Yet, his case would have gone almost unnoticed had it not been for his family, his wife Lucie and his brother Mathieu. They believe in Alfred's innocence already before proof can be given, and step by step they mobilize public opinion. One year after the trial the family as well as the military leadership know who the traitor is: Captain Esterhazy, a well-known gambler. Under normal circumstances Alfred Dreyfus would have been quickly retried and acquitted of any guilt. But since he was a Jew the first trial had been based not only on wrong accusations but moreover on falsification of evidence.

Against the advice of a few officers, among them Picquart, later French Minister of War, a huge cover-up operation is started by the current Minister of War Mercier. "Right or wrong – the Army" is the philosophy behind it. Alfred Dreyfus, being a Jew, the army finds strong allies in the growing anti-Semitic movement, in the high bureaucracy, in conservative circles and not least in the Catholic Church. Apart from the family and a few friends, the campaign for Alfred's rehabilitation is at first only supported by left wing pacifists. Finally, the Affair develops into a big political case: Emile Zola, writer and human rights activist, comes out in favour of the innocent and is followed by many, among them Georges Clemenceau, the famous Prime Minister of later years. Eventually France, her public opinion and her political class are deeply divided between "Dreyfusards" and "Anti-Dreyfusards".

So are Europe, the rest of the world and, last but not least, the Jewish communities. The Zionist movement starts from here, since Theodor Herzl's vision of a future Jewish nation state is published in 1896 after Herzl has attended the first Dreyfus trial as a journalist. Most Jews in Europe and elsewhere, including the Dreyfus family, however, turn their backs on the Zionist ideas. They continue to believe in the possibility of being good Jews and good citizens of their home country at the same time. It takes Hitler and the Shoah to break this belief. This is another reason why even today the Dreyfus Affair is regarded with mixed feelings by many Jews. Not that they hesitate to identify the model character of the Affair as described by Hannah Arendt. But their conclusion is to base their trust – if they are trustful – more in the state of Israel than on the European nation states. Events in Russia and elsewhere during the past decades do strengthen their point.

Not only within the Jewish communities, but even more in the Christian world, the Affair leaves deep marks. When the French Assemblée Nationale decides in 1905 to separate the State completely from the Church it is the Dreyfusard majority led by Clemenceau who brings this decision about – with repercussions throughout Europe. Also, the international human rights movement springs largely from the Dreyfus Affair, more precisely from the long and bitter fight for the rights of an innocent person against the power of the State.

And Alfred Dreyfus, the hero against his own will? He gets his retrial after five years of suffering, only to be convicted again due to false evidence. He accepts a pardon by the President of France. He continues to work, together with his family and friends, for his full rehabilitation, and is successful in 1906 after another six years. Emile Zola who in 1898 had been sentenced to prison and thereby forced into illegal emigration to Britain has died four years before under mysterious circumstances. Only as late as 1908, will he be honoured by being officially reburied in the Paris Pantheon.

At this point, Alfred Dreyfus, the anti-hero, has left centre again in order to live more or less peacefully – except for an attempt on his life – and to serve during World War I as an almost anonymous French officer. When he passes away in 1935, Hitler has already established his regime and decrees the infamous Nuremberg Laws against the Jews in Germany that same year. His wife Lucie must lead a hidden life during the German occupation of France and thus escapes the murderers and can enjoy liberation before she dies in peace. Their grandchild Madeleine can not escape; she was gassed in Auschwitz. The Dreyfus family tried to keep the Affair hidden. But nobody can escape history.

That is why the Dreyfus Affair until today catches, time and again, the attention and imagination of the public at large. Therefore George R. Whyte and his colleagues decided some years ago to present the Affair to the world through artistic and literary means on the occasion of the hundredth anniversary of the first Dreyfus trial. As a result, the *Dreyfus Trilogy* saw the limelight: the opera premiered in Berlin, the danced drama first presented in Bonn, the musical satire shown on TV in Great Britain, France and Germany.

Many other events during the Dreyfus Centenary of 1994 would deserve to be mentioned. Universities in many countries held symposia and seminars; books were published, TV films produced; international youth meetings gathered; newspapers, weeklies and monthlies carried many articles about the Affair and its aftermath. To me, the Dreyfus Opera now to be presented by the New York City Opera at Lincoln Centre was the focal event of the Dreyfus Centenary two years ago. Its message is that of the Affair and of the whole Trilogy: The Shoah can happen again, and everybody is asked to do his or her utmost so that it will never happen again. Tua res agitur: This is your cause, your duty, your responsibility.

Barthold C. Witte, a retired diplomat, is the chairman of the German Dreyfus Society and the German Dreyfus Committee.

AUTHOR'S FOREWORD

Dreyfus, the first Jewish deportee, survived. Within fifty years six million others did not. Fifty years later, ethnic cleansing, racial violence and neo-fascist movements are recurring in both their subtle and deadly forms.

The Dreyfus Trilogy inspired by the Dreyfus Affair deals with one of the scourges of mankind. The hatred for a minority which is perceived as different; the hatred which is sometimes supported by the law of the land; the hatred which leads to persecution, death and genocide. And, the eternal struggle for justice.

The Trilogy in its texts and its treatment deals with evil by demonstrating evil; it deals with bigotry by demonstrating bigotry; it deals with hatred by demonstrating hatred. The works do not flinch from the truth and meticulous care has been exercised to ensure that the texts and the treatments do not distort that truth in any way – however painful or discomforting that truth may be.

Inevitably, some of the material has caused controversy. On a first encounter it can be found shocking and offensive. And if so, that is a vindication of the works which in the final analysis constitute a warning. Such controversy occurred time and again during their realisation and included here are some of the responses and reactions of those involved as and when they occurred.

"Beware, it can happen again" which was a warning phrase at the outset has alas become "Beware it is happening again". The experience of reliving in a dramatised form the events of history; the experience of feeling the horrors and the pain; the theatrical experience of seeing fact and not fiction is intended to contribute to a process of guidance especially for the young and inspire them to enlist in the cause of justice. This is the hope of all those involved in the creation of the Trilogy and all those who unhesitatingly supported these creations based on truth for, in Zola's words, "justice resides in truth alone".

ALFRED DREYFUS

When the right of a
single individual is injured,
the right of all is in peril,
the right of the nation itself.

Georges Clemenceau

J'Accuse…!

LETTRE AU PRÉSIDENT DE LA RÉPUBLIQUE

Par ÉMILE ZOLA

J'accuse

LETTRE

A M. FÉLIX FAURE

Président de la République

Monsieur le Président,

Emile Zola

Lettre à M. Félix Faure
Président de la République

701

Monsieur le Président,

Me permettez-vous, dans ma gratitude pour le bienveillant accueil que vous m'avez fait un jour, d'avoir le souci de votre juste gloire, et de vous dire que votre étoile, si heureuse jusqu'ici, est menacée de la plus honteuse, de la plus ineffaçable des taches?

Vous êtes sorti sain et sauf des basses calomnies, vous avez conquis les cœurs. Vous apparaissez rayonnant dans l'apothéose de cette fête patriotique que l'alliance russe a été pour la France, et vous vous préparez à présider au solennel triomphe de notre Exposition

PRINCIPAL CHARACTERS

CAPTAIN ALFRED DREYFUS

Born in Mulhouse on 9 October 1859 to Jeannette and Raphael Dreyfus, industrialist, the seventh and youngest child; the Alsatian Jewish family embarks on a course of assimilation, loosening its ties to Judaism in order to strengthen its ties with France; enters Ecole Polytechnique in 1878; Lieutenant 1882; Captain 1889; at Ecole de Guerre 1890-92; leaves 1892; ninth in his class with a mention of *très bien*; joins general staff of Ministry of War in 1893 where he is the only Jewish officer; marries Lucie Hadamard in 1890; his son Pierre is born in 1891 and his daughter Jeanne in 1893.

LUCIE DREYFUS

Wife of Alfred; born Lucie Hadamard in 1871 and of a more traditional Jewish background than her husband; observes Jewish Holy Days and is dedicated to biblical study; accomplished pianist; exhibits unshakeable loyalty to her husband throughout the Affair; in later life devotes much of her time to Jewish causes.

EMILE ZOLA

French novelist born in Paris in 1840; family of Italian origin; begins to take interest in the plight of Dreyfus in 1897 and his articles appear in rapid succession with *Lettre à la Jeunesse* in December 1897 and *Lettre à la France* on 6 January 1898; his letter to the President of France, entitled *J'Accuse* appears in *L'Aurore* on 13 January 1898 accusing the General Staff of conspiracy to convict Dreyfus; tried for libel and convicted in February 1898 and sentenced to a fine and one year in prison; he takes refuge in Britain; he dies 'mysteriously' of asphyxiation at his home in 1902; his remains are transferred to the Pantheon in 1908.

EDOUARD DRUMONT

Born 1844; anti-Semitic leader and writer; writes *La France Juive* in 1886, a tirade against Jews that sells 200000 copies; forms National Anti-Semitic League in 1899; launches the Catholic *La Libre Parole* in 1892 with a violent campaign against Jews and their admission into the army; becomes the leading organ of anti-Semitism and anti-Dreyfusard propaganda during the Affair; labelled the Pope of anti-Semitism; dies in 1917.

LIEUTENANT-COLONEL
MARIE-GEORGES PICQUART

Born in Strasbourg in 1854; Saint Cyr; Ecole de Guerre; outstanding officer; exhibits anti-Semitic traits; promoted Head of Counter-Intelligence in 1895; Lieutenant-Colonel in 1896; becomes suspicious of Esterhazy and denounces him; as a result falls into conflict with his senior officers Generals Boisdeffre and Gonse; relieved of his duties in February 1898; arrested in July 1898 and incarcerated at La Santé and then Cherche-Midi Prison until June 1899; re-integrated into the army with the rank of general in 1906 following the rehabilitation of Dreyfus; appointed Minister of War in the Clemenceau Government in 1906; multilingual of exceptional intellect; accomplished musician and pianist; forms Mahler Society; dies in 1914 from a riding accident.

MATHIEU DREYFUS

Brother of Alfred Dreyfus; born 1857; industrialist; elegant and of distinguished bearing; from 1894 devotes his life to the rehabilitation of his brother Alfred; advertises handwriting of 'bordereau' and is contacted by the banker Castro who identifies it as that of his client Esterhazy; he denounces Esterhazy as the author of the 'bordereau'.

JULES GUERIN

Active anti-Semite; supported by the Duc d'Orléans;
founds the Ligue Antisémitique in 1897; publishes
L'Antijuif; masterminds
street violence with his
People's Army; establishes
his headquarters at Fort Chabrol in Paris and is
eventually disgraced.

MAJOR HUBERT-JOSEPH HENRY

Born 1846; volunteers for
the army in 1865; becomes
Second Lieutenant in 1870
and Captain in 1879; wounded in the Franco-Prussian
War; Legion d'Honneur 1895; Lieutenant-Colonel
1897; gives false testimony at first Dreyfus trial and
creates forgeries to strengthen the army's case
against Dreyfus; confesses to the forgeries during
intensive interrogation by Minister of War
Cavaignac on 30 August 1898; found dead in his
prison cell the following day.

MARIE-CAUDRON BASTIAN

Becomes cleaner at the
German Embassy in Paris
in 1889 and eventually the
concierge; works as agent
for French Army Intelli-
gence in particular pas-
sing fragments of documents and papers found in
wastepaper baskets at the embassy for 200 francs
per month; in contact with Henry to whom she
passes the 'bordereau'.

MARIE-CHARLES-FERDINAND WALSIN ESTERHAZY

Born in Paris in 1847;
illegitimate descendant
bearing the name of the
Esterhazy family; becomes
Papal Guard and then joins
the Foreign Legion; marries in 1887 the daughter
of the Marquis de Nettancourt; always in financial
difficulties; takes Marie Pays a young prostitute as
his mistress; calls on Schwartzkoppen in 1894 to
offer his services; is relieved of duty after Henry's
confession of forgeries on 30 August 1898; escapes
to England and admits writing the 'bordereau'; he
lives in England under the name of Count Jean de
Voilement and dies in Harpenden, Kent in 1923;
receives regular sums at the local post office, from
an unknown source.

COLONEL MAXIMILIAN VON SCHWARTZKOPPEN

Born in 1850 in Potsdam;
enters the Infantry Regi-
ment of Westphalia in 1868;
participates in the Franco-
Prussian War 1870; Captain
in 1882; Commandant 1888; appointed Military
Attaché at German Embassy in Paris 1891; has contact with Esterhazy from 1894; participates in the
First World War as Commander of the 20th Infantry Division; dies from wounds in hospital in Berlin
1917 affirming the innocence of Dreyfus whom he
had never met.

MARQUIS
DU PATY
DE CLAM

Born 1853; General Staff
Officer; designated as Officer of Judiciary Police on 14
October 1894; masterminds
enquiry against Dreyfus
and invents the scenario of his hostile interrogation and handwriting test; Lieutenant-Colonel in
1896; participates in intrigues with Esterhazy on
behalf of the Military; theatrical personality; dies
in 1916. Son appointed head of Jewish Bureau under Vichy government.

GENERAL RAOUL
FRANÇOIS CHARLES
LE MOUTON
DE BOISDEFFRE

Born 1839; Army Chief of
Staff from 1893 to 1898;
fervent Catholic; ignores Picquart's protesta-
tions; resigns after Henry's confession of forgeries; dies 1919.

GENERAL
AUGUSTE
MERCIER

Born in 1833; participates
in the campaigns of Mexico
and Metz; Colonel in 1883;
General de Brigade in 1885;
becomes Minister of War in
1894; masterminds creation of sham secret dossier
handed furtively to the judges at the first Dreyfus
court-martial to influence their decision; gives
virulent anti-Dreyfus testimony in Rennes; remains
implacable foe of Dreyfus until the end of his life;
dies in Paris in 1921.

GENERAL
CHARLES-ARTHUR
GONSE

Born 1838; Deputy Chief of
Staff; strong anti-Dreyfus-
ard; friend of Boisdeffre; refuses to listen to
Picquart's evidence against Esterhazy; replaced
after Henry's confession; dies 1917.

MARGUERITE-
MARIE PAYS

Young and attractive prostitute from the provinces
whom Esterhazy reputedly
met on a train journey to
Paris or at the Moulin Rouge;
is already well-known in her
profession at the age of 19; intelligent and loyal to
Esterhazy; becomes his mistress.

CHRONOLOGY

RELATING TO THE DREYFUS AFFAIR

THE ROOTS

70   *Fall of Jerusalem and destruction of the Temple followed by the mass exodus of Jews from the Land of Israel.*

1–4th centuries *Rise of Christianity; anti-Jewish doctrines; charges of deicide and Satanism lay foundation of anti-Jewish stereotype.*

4–10th centuries *Expansion of Christianity throughout Europe; Catholicism promoted as the one true faith; domination of Papacy; discrimination against Jews and their exclusion from guilds; persecution of Jews sanctioned by Canon and Civil Law.*

11–17th centuries *The Crusades; destruction of Jewish communities; anti-Jewish terror throughout Christian Europe; Jews accused of ritual murder and poisoning of wells; burning at the stake and widespread massacres; anti-Jewish stereotype ineradicably embedded into Christian culture; burning of synagogues and Jewish Holy Books; the Inquisition; political domination of Christianity; mass expulsion of Jews from most European countries; establishment of ghettos; Reformation; temporary decrease in persecution in Protestant lands; Luther publishes anti-Semitic tract.*

BACKGROUND TO THE AFFAIR

1749 Birth of Abraham Israel Dreÿfuss recorded in Rixheim.

1791 Declaration of Human Rights; increasing emancipation of Jews; growing anti-Jewish prejudice at all levels of society.

1835 Jacob Dreÿfuss moves to Mülhausen after anti-Jewish incidents in Rixheim.

1848 Anti-Jewish demonstration in Alsace.

1850 Wagner publishes anti-Semitic tract to be followed by Gobinau, Marr, Treitschke, Dühring, Drumont, etc. establishing racial, intellectual and economic basis of anti-Semitism; beginning of modern and political anti-Semitism.

Dreyfus in front of his judges.

THE AFFAIR

HISTORICAL BACKGROUND

1859 Alfred Dreyfus born in Mulhouse to an Alsatian Jewish family.

1870 The young boy Dreyfus vows to become a soldier as he watches the German Army march into Mulhouse during the Franco-Prussian War.

1871 Alsace-Lorraine is annexed by Germany.

1872 The Dreyfus family opts for French nationality and after a brief stay in Basle transfers to Paris.

1880 Lieutenant Dreyfus graduates from the Ecole Polytechnique.

1886 The anti-Semite Edouard Drumont publishes *La France Juive*.

1890 Captain Dreyfus marries Lucie Hadamard.

The degradation of Alfred Dreyfus.

1891 Colonel Schwartzkoppen appointed Military Attaché at the German Embassy in Paris.

1892 Dreyfus completes two year course at the Ecole Superieure de Guerre. Drumont launches the Catholic newspaper *La Libre Parole* and denounces Jews in the army.

1893 Dreyfus becomes probationer on the general staff and the only Jewish officer there.

1894 Dreyfus transferred to Army Intelligence. General Mercier appointed Minister of War.

Commotion in the Chambre des deputés in Paris.

Dreyfus in the Cherche-Midi Military Prison.

THE CONDEMNATION

1894 July Major Esterhazy pays first visit to Schwartzkoppen at the German Embassy and offers his services as a spy.

September 1 'Bordereau' arrives at German Embassy.

End September 'Bordereau' via Bastian arrives at Army Counter-Intelligence.

October 14 General Mercier orders handwriting test of Dreyfus but signs warrant for his arrest before the result is known.

October 15 Dreyfus is arrested and incarcerated in the Cherche-Midi Military Prison, Paris.

December 19–21 Court martial of Dreyfus conducted in camera. Henry denounces Dreyfus. Secret dossier passed by the Military to the judges without the knowledge of the defence.

December 22 Dreyfus found guilty and condemned to public degradation, exile and imprisonment for life.

1895 January 5 Dreyfus publicly degraded in Paris in the courtyard of the Ecole Militaire in front of his fellow officers and a hysterical mob. First public signs of violent anti-Semitism. Theodor Herzl reporting for the *Neue Freie Presse* in Vienna is alarmed.

April 13 Dreyfus arrives on Devil's Island.

THE YEARS OF DEPORTATION

1895 July 1 Picquart appointed head of Army Counter Intelligence.

1896 February 14 Theodor Herzl publishes in Vienna *Judenstaat*, advocating the establishment of a Jewish national homeland.

August Picquart identifies Esterhazy as author of 'bordereau'.

September 1 Picquart advises Boisdeffre of Esterhazy's guilt. He is rejected.

September 3 Dreyfus on Devil's Island is placed in double shackles.

September 15 Picquart meets Gonse and recommends arrest of Esterhazy. He is rejected.

November 10 *Le Matin* publishes facsimile of 'bordereau'.

November 16 Picquart ordered away from Paris.

1897 February Supported by the Duc d'Orléans, Jules Guérin organises the Ligue Antisémitique Française.

November 15 Mathieu advertises 'bordereau' publicly.

November 25 Zola publishes his first article in support of Dreyfus.

December 13 Zola publishes *Letter to Youth* calling on young intellectuals to support Dreyfus.

Colonel Jouast, president of the Conseil de guerre in Rennes.

Dreyfus at the Rennes trial.

Confrontation of Henry and Picquart.

January 24 Von Bülow declares in Reichstag that Germany never had contact with Dreyfus.

February 7–23 Zola tried for libel and declared guilty. Fined 30 000 francs and sentenced to one year in prison; later flees to England.

February 26 Picquart dismissed from the Army.

February 28 Lucie Dreyfus requests permission to go to Devil's Island but is refused.

March 4 Picquart – Henry duel. Henry slightly wounded.

July 7 Minister of War Cavaignac unknowingly reads one of Henry's forgeries to the Chamber of Deputies, as a proof of Dreyfus' guilt.

July 9 Picquart challenges Cavaignac's proof.

July 13 Picquart arrested.

August 30 Henry confesses to forging documents and is imprisoned.

August 31 Henry found dead in his prison cell.

September 1 Esterhazy flees to England.

September 3 Cavaignac resigns; Lucie Dreyfus petitions for a re-trial.

December 15 Mathieu Dreyfus denounces Esterhazy as the author of the 'bordereau' in open letter to the Ministry of War.

1898 January 7 Zola publishes *Letter to France*.

January 10–11 Esterhazy is given a sham trial before a court-martial and acquitted.

January 13 Emile Zola publishes *J'accuse* in *L'Aurore*.

January 17 Anti-Semitic riots throughout France; Jules Guérin's People's Army active; Jewish homes and synagogues besieged; shops broken; incidents in Nantes, Bordeaux, Montpellier, Tours, Toulouse; Dreyfus effigies burnt; demonstrations in Marseille, Nancy and all of Lorraine; religious services held to continue the "sacred battle" against the Jews; in Algeria synagogues ransacked; Jews stoned.

Duel of Picquart and Henry.

The handwriting expert Bertillon in front of the Conseil de guerre in Rennes.

THE RETRIAL

1899 June 3 United Court of Appeal revokes 1894 verdict and orders Dreyfus to be retried by court-martial in Rennes.

June 5 Zola returns to France.

June 9 Dreyfus sails to France; Picquart freed.

August 7 to September 9 Rennes Trial. Dreyfus declared guilty again and condemned to public degradation and 10 years imprisonment.

September 19 At the instigation of his family who fear for his survival, Dreyfus accepts pardon to enable him to prove his innocence.

September 21 Dreyfus arrives in Carpentras.

1900 April 14 Exposition Universelle in Paris.

1902 Publication in Russia of *The Protocols of the Elders of Zion*; Polish and Russian pogroms continue, heralding widespread massacres of Jewish communities.

September 2 Zola dies mysteriously at home from asphyxiation.

THE REHABILITATION

1903 April 4 Jean Jaurès demands in the Chamber of Deputies revision of Rennes verdict.

1905 French legislation separates Church and State.

1906 July 12 The Supreme Court of Appeal in Paris annuls the Rennes verdict and declares Dreyfus innocent of all the charges against him.

July 13 Parliament votes to reinstate Dreyfus and Picquart into the Army.

July 21 Dreyfus is awarded the Legion of Honour at public ceremony.

October 15 Dreyfus resumes military duties.

October 25 Clemenceau becomes Prime Minister. Picquart is appointed Minister of War.

EPILOGUE

1908 *June 4* Zola's ashes are transferred to the Pantheon; attempt on the life of Dreyfus during the ceremony; culprit is acquitted.

1914 *January 19* Picquart dies in a riding accident.

July 31 Jean Jaurès assassinated.

August 2 Dreyfus returns to active duty, promoted Lieutenant-Colonel and serves in First World War.

1922 Walter Rathenau, Jewish Foreign Minister of Germany, assassinated by racist extremists.

1931 *February* The play *L'Affaire Dreyfus* by Rehfisch and Herzog staged in Paris; violent demonstrations; injuries and arrests.

1935 *July 12* Death of Alfred Dreyfus; buried in the Cemetery of Montparnasse in Paris.

Dreyfus – The wandering Jew.

THE AFTERMATH

1935 *Nuremberg laws enacted.*

1938 *'Reichskristallnacht'.*

1939 *Commencement of Second World War.*

1940 *First Vichy Statut des Juifs.*

1942 *Wannsee conference.*
Deportation of French Jews to Auschwitz begins.

1943 *Granddaughter of Dreyfus deported from Drancy to Auschwitz where she perishes.*

1945 *War ends.*
Death of Lucie Dreyfus.
Figure for genocide of Jews becomes known and totals 6 million.

1946 *Polish pogroms; Jews murdered.*
Nuremberg trials.

1948 *Establishment of the State of Israel.*

1962–65 *Vatican II rejects anti-Jewish teachings.*

1970 *First signs of anti-Semitism cloaked as anti-Zionism.*

1980 *Bombing of Paris Synagogue.*

1988 *Erection of statue to Dreyfus in the Jardin de Tuileries; desecration of the grave of Dreyfus in the cemetery of Montparnasse.*

1990 *Marked increase of anti-Semitic acts throughout Europe.*
Desecration of Jewish cemetery in Carpentras.

1994 *Dreyfus Centenary commemorations.*
Dismissal of French Army historian Colonel Paul Gaujac for questioning innonence of Dreyfus.
Bombing of Jewish Centre in Buenos Aires, killing 100 people.
Increase of anti-Semitic acts in Italy.
Increase of anti-Semitic acts in Russia.
Increase of anti-Semitic acts in the Ukraine.
Increase of anti-Semitic acts in Lithuania.
Increase of anti-Semitic acts in Germany.
Arson attack on Lübeck Synagogue.
Desecration of Buchenwald Memorial.
Increase of anti-Semitic acts in France.
Desecration of cemeteries in Alsace Lorraine.
Desecration of Drancy Memorial.
.....

ADMISSION IS NOT ACCEPTANCE I

AN HISTORIC INJUSTICE

"Death to the Jews" drowned the protests of Alfred Dreyfus during his public degradation as he was stripped of his rank, his honour and, ironically, the very ideals which had guided his life – love of the army and devotion to the patrie. His calvary was to last twelve years and the Dreyfus Affair it precipitated was to become one of the most troubled periods in the history of France, recording for future generations a far-seeing testimony of the social turbulence of the times.

The defeat of France in the Franco-Prussian War dealt a grievous blow to the pride of the nation. The army became the sacred instrument of revenge. It would recapture the lost territories and regain France's honour. It was revered. It was beyond reproach. It was a hallowed institution.

Conversely, the influx of foreigners into France met with increasing antagonism from the population. The country was being invaded by vagabonds, peddlers and upstarts. In an atmosphere of growing xenophobia, the people resented this 'pollution' of their land. The theme of *Those without a Country* was to be heard again and again counterpointed with *France for the French.*

Anti-Semitism, always lurking within a Christian culture, gathered pace when the writer Edouard Drumont, who was to become the "Pope of anti-Semitism", arrived on the scene. The Catholic Church and its organ *La Croix* had long maintained an anti-Jewish stance and the venom of Drumont would drive their bigotry to fever pitch. "To be French was to be Catholic". Protestants, Freemasons and above all the Jews were suspect.

These three undercurrents, love of the army, suspicion of the foreigner and mistrust of the Jew would converge in the Dreyfus Affair and burst the dams of all social restraint, creating a torrent of hate on an unprecedented scale.

The conviction of Alfred Dreyfus left many minds unconvinced. The Jewish thinker, Bernard Lazare, was soon to publish his clandestine pamphlet in Belgium. Lucie Dreyfus, the loyal wife and Mathieu, the 'good' brother began their odyssey for evidence to exonerate Alfred. Theodor Herzl, horrified by the mass hysteria at the degradation, went on to write *Judenstaat*, a manifesto for a Jewish homeland. Emile Zola, increasingly convinced that there had been a miscarriage of justice began to voice his doubts and his articles appeared in rapid succession. He deplored that young minds had already been infected by the poison of anti-Semitism. "What trepidation for the approaching century". He implored the youth of France:

Oh Youth! Youth!
I beg you consider the great task which awaits
you. You are the architects of the future.
Youth! Youth!
Remain always on the side of justice.
If the concept of justice were to fade within
your soul, you will be open to grave dangers.
Youth! Youth!
Be humane. Be generous.

"Where are you heading young people"? he asked "towards humanity, truth and justice" Zola exclaimed. He was to be ridiculed, mocked and caricatured, but became the eloquent spokesman for the cause of justice.

The Jews of France had been stunned into silence, fearing that the shame of one would be visited on them all. In happier days, as Alfred

Dreyfus adjusted his uniform every morning he saw in his mirror the reflection of a proud French Officer. When he arrived at General Staff headquarter, he was perceived as a Jewish officer. He did not see, or want to see, that admission was not acceptance. This was the bitter lesson to be learned from the misfortunes of the assimilationist officer. Jews throughout the world mourned the fate of yet one more Jewish martyr while Dreyfus, lingering in his cell on Devil's Island, clutching a small photo of his wife and children, his talisman, ravaged by disease and depression, tortured with double shackles, tried to hold on to life.

Then came the bombshell, *J'Accuse*. The sham trial and acquittal of the suspected traitor Esterhazy incensed Zola beyond measure. *J'Accuse* roared across the headlines of the newspaper *L'Aurore* on 30 January 1898 to become the watershed of the Dreyfus Affair. The anti-Dreyfusards closed ranks and the knives were out. Zola would be tried and convicted. He would be abused and vilified. Stripped of his Legion d'Honneur, never to be returned, he was the friend of a traitor (whom he had never met), he was a foreigner in the service of an alleged syndicate, he was in the pay of the Jews. Undaunted, he testified at his trial:

Dreyfus is innocent, that I swear. For this I pledge my life for this I pledge my honour.

Before France, before the whole world I swear that Dreyfus is innocent, and by my forty years of work, by the authority this labour has given me, I swear that Dreyfus is innocent. And by all that I have gained, by the name which I have made for myself, by my work which has helped to enrich French literature I swear that Dreyfus is innocent. May all this crumble, may all my work perish if Dreyfus is not innocent!

He is innocent!

The Affair had now reached its explosive phase and would engulf the whole country. Its tremors were to be felt throughout the civilised world. Justice was now on trial on the world stage of human rights. As evidence gathered in favour of Dreyfus, the fight for the retrial was won and the most intensive period of the Affair was unleashed. At Rennes, the site of the second court martial, effigies of Alfred Dreyfus were burnt by uncontrolled mobs. Hatred was mobilised into song with pride of place reserved for the National Hymn converted into *La Marseillaise Antijuive*:

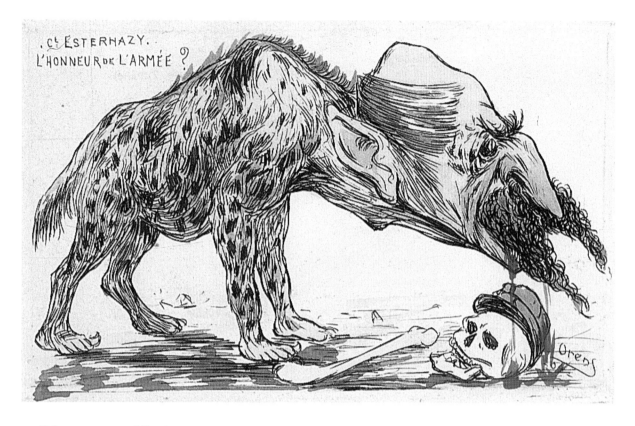

Take up arms anti-Semites!
Form your batallions!
March on! March on!
Let their tainted blood
Drench our fields!
Berlin soon responded with
Dreyfus, Dreyfus über alles:
Holy Dreyfus, innocent heart
Our pride and joy forever
Truthful always. Never false
Purity is your endeavour.
Yes – to wallow in men's blood
From your foot to the horns on your head
And to betray the whole wide world
That is innocence? – what dread!
Endless caricatures, verses and songs were created in an ever more vicious circle of abuse.

The country was in turmoil, society was divided, families were split. Dreyfusards clashed with anti-Dreyfusards. Violence was in the air. Anti-Semitic riots ravaged the cities of France. Synagogues were ransacked, shops were pillaged, people attacked. Back in Paris Jules Guérin, head of the anti-Semitic League was roaming the streets with his People's Army. His headquarters at Fort Chabrol churned out the poisoned pen anti-Semitic *L'Antijuive* and became a veritable factory of venom. A whole catechism of calumnies was disgorged by the anti-Semitic press in an endless series of scurrilous texts as Drumont, at his zenith, prophesied with spine-chilling accuracy:

The Jews have to be eternally blind as they have always been not to realise what is awaiting them. They will be taken away as scrap and the people that they oppress so harshly, that they exploit with such ferocity, will dance with joy when they learn that justice has been done.

The leader who will suddenly emerge incarnating the idea of an entire nation will do whatever pleases him. He will have the right of life and death. He will be able to employ any means that suit his purpose.

Paris in the fog: Demonstrations. – "Death to the Jews !...".

The great organiser who will unite the resentments, anger and suffering, will achieve a result which will resound throughout the universe. He will return to Europe its prestige for 200 years.
Who is to say that he is not already at work?
With the innocent officer found guilty again at Rennes the anti-Dreyfusards were vindicated but world opinion was outraged. Zola was aghast:

I feel terror.
The sacred terror of rivers
Flowing back to their source,
Of the earth
Turning without a sun.
Never has there been a more
Detestable monument of human
Infamy or act of wickedness.
It will make future generations shudder.

Dreyfus, convicted a third time by his pardon, continued the fight until his total exoneration and it is to the everlasting credit of France that justice was finally done. Zola died in 'mysterious' circumstances and was both reviled and honoured in his obituaries. His ashes were eventually transferred to the Pantheon where an attempt was made on the life of Alfred Dreyfus. The culprit was acquitted.

Rumblings of the Affair continued and do to this day. The first war passed, with its horrors, to be surpassed by the second with its atrocities. Members of the Dreyfus family fought valiantly, served in the resistance, died. Nor were the transports from Drancy to Auschwitz to be without a member of the Dreyfus family. The songwriters' predictions were fulfilled. "Take up arms anti-Semites" became a reality as did "Death to the Jews".

RAGE AND OUTRAGE

MUSICAL SATIRE
IN ONE ACT

Sequence 1
THE INNOCENCE OF DREYFUS I

Piano solo

Arrival of participants. Author arrives with images and texts. He circles the words 'Rage' and 'Outrage' and hands letter to the chanteuse who reads text aloud. Piano enters at the end of the third paragraph.

Devil's Island, 5 october 1895
Letter from Alfred Dreyfus to the President of the French Republic.

Accused and then condemned on the evidence of handwriting for the most infamous crime a soldier can commit, I have declared and I declare once again that I never wrote the letter with which I was charged and I have never forfeited my honour.

For a year, I have been struggling alone, conscious of my innocence, in the most terrible circumstances which can befall a man. I do not speak of physical suffering, that is nothing, a broken heart is everything.

To suffer for myself is frightful but to know that those dear to me are suffering on my behalf is unbearable.

My whole family is in torment for an abominable crime which I did not commit.

I do not beg for pardon or favours or even assurances. What I ask is that the light of truth should be shed upon the conspiracy which has made victims of my unhappy family and myself.

(Chanteuse continues to read silently.) Then aloud.

What gives me strength are the thoughts of Lucie and my children.

Ah, my dearest children! I am not afraid to die. But before dying, I would like to know that your names have been cleansed of this filth.

As piano solo ends, chanteuse reads aloud.

12 janvier 1896
Answer from the President of the French Republic.
Rejected, without any comment.

Sequence 2
THE INNOCENCE OF DREYFUS II

Voice and accordion

Original	*Translation*
L'Innocence de Dreyfus	**Innocence of Dreyfus**

Depuis longtemps un soldat de la France	For too many years
souffre un exilé accablé de mé-pris	A soldier of France
pauvre martyre malgré son innocence	Has suffered alone
fut condamné sans rien avoir compris	A martyr condemned
en l'accusant de honte et d'infamie	Abandoned in silence
pour épargner des lâches imposteurs	Shamed and accursed
il fut choisi dans leur ignominie	To save the corrupt
comme victime de bordereau menteur.	And their cowardly plans.

Refrain	*Refrain*
Tu reviendras vaillant martyr de France	One day you'll return, o valiant Frenchman
pauvre exilé banni de ton pays	Wrongly exiled from your native land
souris en fin à ta belle espérance	The beauty of hope will shine upon you
en maudisant les lâches ennemis.	Your dastardly foes forever banned.

Dans son erreur toute la France entière	The whole land of France
a cru pourtant à ces absurdités	Bewildered, misled
Mais il survint un homme de lumière	Was shown the true light
Emile Zola disant la vérité	By Zola
Malgré tous ceux qui lui jettent la pierre	Who, braving the stones
Il a bravé la France avec honneur	Armed only with words
Pour ramener aux orphelins le père	Saved the poor children
Depuis longtemps accablé de douleur.	Their father.

(Refrain)	*(Refrain)*

Sequence 3
THE INNOCENCE OF DREYFUS III

Flute, violin, clarinet and cello. Text over music

DRUMONT When the French have been stripped to the bone, smothered in the excrement and spittle of Jews, refugees, foreigners, beggars and all other stateless ones who have overrun our unfortunate country, Frenchmen will come looking for me and my comrades.

Then we will cleanse this country, as other great men have done before us.

Sequence 4
THE ANTI-JEWISH MARSEILLAISE

Chorus and orchestra

ZOLA The poison is the violent hatred for the Jews which has
been fed to the people every morning for years. There is a
gang of poisoners, and, hear this, they do it in the name of
morality, in the name of Christ, as avengers and dispens-
ers of justice.

Introductory music starts.

ZOLA In these terrible days of moral strife, at a time when public
conscience seems to have darkened, it is to you dear France
that I address myself, to the nation, to the homeland.
What has happened beloved France? How is it that your
people of good heart and good sense have reached these
depths of fear and intolerance?

Original **La Marseillaise Antijuive**	*Translation* **The Anti-Jewish Marseillaise**
Tremblez, youpins, et vous, perfides,	Start trembling Yids and traitors
L'opprobe de tous les partis,	Despised by one and all
Contre nous de la juiverie	If the Jews rise up against us
Le troupeau hurlant s'est levé *(bis)*.	And avenging hordes will roar *(repeat)*.
Français, pour nous, ah! quel outrage	Frenchmen it's an outrage
D'être insultés par ces bandits,	Our weakness has allowed
Balayons donc tous ces youdis	Let's rid ourselves of outlaws
Que notre faiblesse encourage.	May Jews be disavowed.
Aux armes, antijuifs, formez vos bataillons.	To arms anti-Semites! Form your battalions!
Marchons, marchons,	March on, march on
Qu'un sang impur abreuve nos sillons.	May our fields be drenched with their tainted blood.

Eh! quoi cette race pourrie	And how this rotten race
De Dreyfusards, de va-nu-pieds	Of Dreyfus and the likes
Insulterait notre Patrie,	Insult our noble homeland
Ferait la loi dans nos foyers! *(bis)*	Dictating all our lives! *(repeat)*
Aux juifs fais mordre la poussière,	Bite the dust, you Jews, you thieves
Fais rendre gorge à ces voleurs	We'll drive you from our shores
De notre or et de notre honneur	You will not profit from your vice
Puis chasse-les hors la frontière.	Just stay with you and yours.
Aux armes, antijuifs, formez vos bataillons.	To arms anti-Semites! Form your battalions
Marchons, marchons,	March on, march on
Qu'un sang impur abreuve nos sillons.	May our fields be drenched with their tainted blood.

Chanteuse reads aloud, over musical improvisation, extract
of Dreyfus letter from Devil's Island to his wife Lucie.

Such torment finally passes the bounds of human endurance. It renews each day the poignancy of the agony. It crushes an innocent man alive into the tomb.

At times, I am so despairing, so worn out, that I have a longing to lie down and just let my life ebb away. I cannot by my own act hasten the end. I have not, I shall never have that right.

This punishment is beyond endurance.

Sequence 5
FOLKSONG I

Voice and Piano

Original	*Translation*
Volkslied: Was I träumt hab'	**What I dreamt**

Auf ferner, weltverlass'ner Insel	Alone on an island
Sitzt ein Gefangener still	Lost to the world
und denkt:	The lonely prisoner sits.
Ob jemals mir in diesem Leben	When will the country of my soul
Mein Frankreich wohl die Freiheit schenkt!	Accept my innocence?
Und weiter denkt er seines Weibes,	He tenderly thinks
Das treu um ihren Gatten weint,	Of his wife in grief
Da murmelt er in seinem Kerker,	And murmurs
Den selten nur ein Strahl bescheint:	in his dank dark cell:
Weißt du, Frankreich was i träumt hab',	Do you know France what I dreamt
Ich habe in die Zukunft g'sehn.	One day there came a vision
Ich sah mein Weib wie einen Engel,	My beloved, a shining angel
Um Rettung und um Freiheit fleh'n	Lighting up my gloomy prison.
Und du, La France, ließt nicht vergebens	She begged for justice and for freedom
Sie bitten um Gerechtigkeit,	And France, at last you heard her
Ich sah mich wieder an der Seine,	For by the Seine I walked again
Geehrt, wie einst in alter Zeit.	As once I did with honour.

Sequence 6
FOLKSONG II

Clarinet and piano

Chanteuse reads extracts of letters from Alfred Dreyfus on Devil's Island to his wife Lucie.

December 13, 1895
They will certainly end by killing me through repeated sufferings or by forcing me to seek in suicide an escape from insanity.

    Each night I dream of my wife and children. But what terrible awakenings! When I open my eyes and find myself in this hut, I have a moment of such anguish that I could close my eyes forever, never to see or think again.

Thursday September 3, 1896, 9 o'clock, morning
The last boat has come and has not brought my letters!

Tuesday September 8, 1896
My dear little Pierre, my dear little Jeanne, my dear Lucie, – all of you whom I love from the depths of my heart and with all the ardour of my soul, – believe me, if these lines reach you, that I have done everything which is humanly possible to hold out.

Sequence 7
THE YID'S POLKA

Chorus and orchestra

Text read over musical introduction.

DRUMONT One recognises the Jews thus: the celebrated hooked
nose, squinting eyes, clenched teeth, ugly ears and
deformed nails, sagging belly, flat feet, rounded knees, the
ankle poking outwards, the hands sweaty and limp; these
are all signs of the hypocrite and the traitor – they often
have one arm shorter than the other.

Original	*Translation*
La Polka des Youpins	**The Yid's Polka**
V'là qu'dans les rues d'Paris	Here in the streets of Paris
On n'trouve plus qu'des youdis.	Only Yids are to be found
A chaque pas sur votre chemin	At each and every turn
Vous n'voyez qu'des youpins.	Only Yids are seen around
C'est une race de vermine,	Such a race of vermin
Ils ont de tristes mines.	With their pathetic grins
On d'vrait les expulser	Should either be thrown out
Ou bien les assommer.	Or else be done right in.
Tra la la la la	Tra la la la la
La la la la la	La la la la la
Chassez ces coquins	Kick out the dirty Yids
Oh! les sales youpins.	Hip! Hip! Hip! Hurrah!
D'après leurs renseignements	In their twisted minds
Dreyfus est innocent,	Dreyfus is not to blame
Mais ils sont incapables	Although the guilty party
D'découvrir le coupable.	Not one of them can name
On peut l'dire sans vergogne	Their sordid end is nigh
Ils ont triste besogne,	So when their race is gone
Quand leur race périra	We'll celebrate with song
Alors chacun chantera.	Holding our heads up high.
Tra la la la la	Tra la la la la
La la la la la	La la la la la
Chassez ces coquins	Kick out the dirty Yids
Oh! les sales youpins.	Hip! Hip! Hip! Hurrah!

C'est vraiment une sale clique
Qu'ces mangeurs de mastic,
Ils sont fourbes et menteurs,
Orateurs, beaux parleurs,
Ils sont très braves aussi,
Rien que l'jour, pas la nuit,
Mais au premier coup d'feu
Ils s'sauvent à qui mieux mieux.

Tra la la la la
La la la la la
Chassez ces coquins
Oh! les sales youpins.

Ils sont marchands d'assiettes
Ou bien de bicyclettes,
Quoiqu'habitant Paris,
Ce sont des sans-patrie;
Faut chasser cette espèce
A coups d'pied dans les fesses
Chassez tous les youdis!
C'est le cri de Paris.

Tra la la la la
La la la la la
Chassez ces coquins
Oh! les sales youpins.

A really dirty clique
Who speak well and who speak pious
What they eat will make you sick
They're treacherous and liars
Brave by day but not by night
And when a shot is heard
They run off and they disappear
And vanish out of sight.

Tra la la la la
La la la la la
Kick out these dirty Yids
Hip! Hip! Hip! Hurrah!

Paris lodgers no one wants
Peddling plates and bikes
A good kick up their rotten arse
Should rid us of these kikes
Without a home to call their own
They spread themselves around
Down with the Yids. Down with the Yids
Leave Paris well alone.

Tra la la la la
La la la la la
Kick out the dirty Yids
Hip! Hip! Hip! Hurrah!

Sequence 8
FOLKSONG III

Voice and accordion

Original	*Translation*
Volkslied: Was I träumt hab'	**What I dreamt**

Im Arbeitszimmer, da lehnt Zola,	Alone in his study
Des Freundes Schicksal dauert ihn:	Zola sat pondering
Hätt' Flügel er, sie müßten tragen	The fate of his friend
Ihn dahin, wo die Wolken zieh'n,	Has left him wondering
Zu Dreyfus, den er wollt' befreien	If Zola had wings he would fly
Von einem feilen Kriegsgericht,	To free Dreyfus from grief and a lie
Da über ihn, als wie Erleuchtung	Suddenly in blinding light
Es kommt und eine Stimme spricht:	A gentle voice is heard:
Weißt du, Zola, was i träumt hab'	Do you know Zola what I dreamt
Hab' in die Zukunft eini g'sehn,	I looked into the future
Um ihn, den du so sehr beklagtest,	The friend for whom you feel such sorrow
Wird bald der Freiheit Banner weh'n.	Will for sure be freed tomorrow
Unschuldig hat er viel gelitten,	The test of time is at an end
Doch bald ist seine Prüfung aus	A proud ship of France is sailing
Und Frankreichs stolzeste Fregatte	And once again the flag will fly
Geleitet meerwärts ihn nach Haus.	To honour his returning.

DRUMONT No weakness, no pity for the Jews!

Sequence 9
DREYFUS ABOVE ALL I

Orchestra

ZOLA I have already said how this barbaric campaign, which takes us back a thousand years, arouses my craving for brotherhood, my passion for tolerance and human equality.

DRUMONT These are people who have always, under every regime, in every corner of the earth, whether it be in relationship to Muslims or Christians, been the object of the same insults and the same hatreds. How do you explain all that?

ZOLA To return once again to the wars of religion and persecution – to wish to exterminate one another, race by race is so utterly senseless that, in this century of enlightenment, such a concept is only for imbeciles.

DRUMONT Yes, our day is coming, but alas in the middle of the storm.

If we were overthrown, every word that we have uttered, every word that evoked the derision of the press would explode with sudden fury and "The Jews – it is the Jews!" would take on a terrible meaning. For the French once again, the end would justify the means.

ZOLA And I refuse to believe that such a movement could once again prosper in this country of free thought, brotherly love and clear intellect.

Sequence 10
PRISONER'S LAMENT

Voice and orchestra

Original
Пѣснь Узника

Невинно я на островѣ томлюся
Враги хотятъ погибели моей!
За честь свою я смерти не страшуся
Семью мнѣ жаль, страшна разлука съней!
Тоска и скорбь мнѣ сердце сильно гложутъ
Поруганъ я отчизпою своей!
Но правды свѣтъ мнѣ другъ пролить поможетъ
Семью мнѣ жаль тяжка разлука съ ней.
Огонь горитъ Въ груди,
Отвагой сердце бьется
Отчизну ли свою спасти
Страданье мнѣ дается?
Пусть всѣ клянутъ меня,
Меня ли жизнь прельшаетъ?
Судьба моя, всего меня
Лишь вѣрой насышаетъ.

Phonetic Transcription
p'esn'j uznj'ika

nevi n n o y a n a ostrove tom l'yusiya
vragnj k'hotiat pogibel'i moey
za tchest'j svoyou ya smert'ine strash-yousiya
semiyou mn'je shal'j strashna razlooka s n'ej
toska i skorb'j mne serdtse sil'jno gloz'joot
paroogan ya otchiznouyou svoyey
no pravdy svet mn'je droug prolit'j pomoshet
sem'you mn'je shal'j t'jashka razlouka s n yey
ogon'j gorit v groud'ji
otvagoy serdtse byjotsya
otchiznoo l'i svoyoo spaste
stradan'jie mn'je daetsya
poust'j vs'je klyanoot men'ya
men'ya l'i zjizn'j prel'jshtchaet?
sood'jba moya, vsevo moya
l'ish v'yerouy nasishchaet.

Translation
Prisoner's Lament

All innocent I suffer on this island
My enemies wish only for my death
Though unafraid to perish for my honour
Grieving for loved ones cannot be endured.
Yearning and sadness devastate my spirit
Honour and trust no longer my birthright
My motherland deserts her faithful soldier
Still I rely on truth to show the light.
Heartsick to be apart
My brain's on fire, my heart courageous
How can this penance redeem my country
My fate a lifetime of oppression.
True faith is my support
Life means no more to me than longing
Despised, rejected, my soul in torment
Branded a traitor to my land.

ZOLA Dreyfus is innocent, that I swear. For this I pledge my life, for this I pledge my honour.

Before France, before the whole world I swear that Dreyfus is innocent and by my forty years of work, by the authority this labour has given me, I swear that Dreyfus is innocent. And by all that I have gained, by the name which I have made for myself, by my work which has helped to enrich French literature, I swear that Dreyfus is innocent. May all this crumble, may all my work perish if Dreyfus is not innocent!

He is innocent!

Sequence 11
INTERROGATION OF DREYFUS

Voices, strings, two accordions and piano

Original
L'Interrogatoire de Dreyfus

Accusé, votre nom, votre âge ?	
Mon colonel, je n`en sais rien !	
Vous êt's inculpé d'espionnage	
Avec l'Etat-Major Prussien.	
Dit's la vérité.	
Toutc la vérité !	

Non, dit Dreyfus impertubable,
Colonel, on vous a trompé
J'vous jur' que je n'suis pas coupable.
Le Rabbin m'a déjà coupé !

Au Ministère de la Guerre,
Quand arriva le bordereau,
Vous étiez officier stagiaire
D'puis qué'qu'temps au deuxièm'bureau ;
Dit's la vérité,
Rien qu'la vérité ;

Mon président, j'suis pas coupable,
Ça, c'est la faute aux généraux
Qui ont dit : Faut prouver, que diable !
Qu'c'est Dreyfus qu'a fait l'bordereau.

On vous a vu, ce n'est pas niable,
Fureter toujours et partout ;
Vous vouliez, s'pèce d'misérable,
Renseigner les All'mands sur tout !
Dit's la vérité,
Rien q'la vérité.

Mon colonel, je vais vouz dire :
Je cherchais c'qu'on n'peut pas trouver,
Car c'était, non d'une tirlire,
Un youpin qu'a pas un grand nez.

Translation
The Interrogation of Dreyfus

Accused, your name, what is your age ?
Sir, I do not know
You stand charged with espionage
For the Prussian foe
Tell the truth
The whole truth !

No Sir, says haughty Dreyfus
In fact you've been misled
Where the Rabbi cut me
My honour grew instead.

A document arrived
At the Ministry of War
Where you, a Junior Officer
Served in the Intelligence Corps
Tell the truth
The whole truth !

Sir, I am not guilty
The generals are to blame
They said Go to the Devil
It's they who bear the shame.

We know that you were seen
Ferreting high and low
You wanted, worthless wretch
To aid the German foe
Tell the truth
The whole truth !

Sir, I will now tell you
I looked and searched and chose
Impossible it was to find
An unhooked Jewish nose.

Vous étiez un trist' personnage.
Coureur de femme et de tripot,
Et rien qu'pour vot'dévergondage
On eut dû vous f...iche à l'hostot.
Dit's la vérité,
Rien q'la vérité.

Mon colonel, malgré ma bille,
Qu'a pas l'air de vous amuser,
J'avais qu'une All'mand' très gentille,
Qui m'app'lait: Sa p'tit crott' sucrée.

Maintenant, la preuve est bien faite,
Vous êt's un officier félon,
Vous avez touché d'la galette,
Comme prix de vot' trahison;
V'là la vérité,
Tout' la vérité;

Non, dit Dreyfus imperturbable.
Colonel, on vous a trompé
J'vous jur' que je n'suis pas coupable,
Le Rabbin m'a déjà coupé!

La Moral' de cett' triste histoire,
C'est qu'malgré l'argent des vauriens,
Malgré l'Syndicat, la victoire
Ne restera pas aux youpins,
Ces oiseaux d'malheurs,
Traîtres ou voleurs;
Et chacun reprendra confiance,
Quand tous ces sal's juifs parvenus
Seront chassés de notre France
A grands coups de savat's dans l'cul.

You were a sorry figure
A philanderer and cheat
You should have been disposed of
Leaving us clean and neat
Tell the truth
Nothing but the truth!

Sir, I swear despite my beak
Which doesn't seem to please you
One day a German girl I took
Who called me her sweet poo-poo...

Such proof will not acquit
An officer and felon
Who had his just rewards
As payment for high treason
That is the truth
The whole truth!

No Sir, says haughty Dreyfus
In fact you've been misled
Where the Rabbi cut me
My honour grew instead.

The moral of this story
I shall now gladly tell
Despite their dirty money
The Yids will go to Hell
These thieves and wicked traitors
These lousy birds of prey
A good kick up their bums
Will make them go away
So dear France, be thankful
Now – let us go and pray.

Sequence 12
COMMENT/DREYFUS ABOVE ALL II

Clarinet and two accordions

DRUMONT The Jew is the most powerful trouble-maker the
world has ever produced and he goes through life joyous-
ly causing harm to Christians. How happy many would
be to unsheath their swords and defend what the Jews
defile – Christ, the Church and our Homeland!

ZOLA It is a poison. This rabid hatred of the Jews which is fed
to the people every morning in the name of morality, in the
name of Christ. It is a very simple ploy to fan the fires of
anti-Semitic rage. What a triumph. Is this not the basis of
the dogma to rekindle once again the intolerance of the
Middle Ages to burn the Jews?

Voice, piano and doublebass

Original	*Translation*
Dreyfus über alles	**Dreyfus above all**
Heil'ger Dreyfus, Unschuldsseele,	Holy Dreyfus, innocent heart
Stolz und Stern des ganzen Seins,	Our pride and joy forever
Ohne Falsch und ohne Fehler	Truthful always, never false
Ist Dein Herz, so rein wie kein's!	Purity is your endeavour
Nie durchdringt ja Deine Kehle	Your soul sustains a life so fine
Nur ein Bissen Fleisch des Schwein's,	No lying and no error
Daß nichts Unreines sich stehle	Pig-meat does not pass your lips
In ein Herz, so rein wie Dein's!	The thought fills you with terror.
Zola steh' Dir treu zur Seite	Let Zola stand close by your side
Mit Reklameschmiererei'n,	While all the world observes
Um des Erdballs Läng' und Breite	To cheat the good and simple folk
Gründlich noch zu seifen ein!	His famous words he serves
Bis in Abram's Schoß geleite	To Abraham he'll shepherd you
Er Dich einst aus Not und Pein,	And help relieve your sufferance
Und des Universums Weite	The universe is large enough to
Mög' dann Euer Spucknapf sein!	hear each filthy utterance.

ZOLA It is a crime to accuse of agitation those,
who wish France to be generous
It is a crime to poison the young and the simple
It is a crime to exploit patriotism for deeds of hatred
It is a crime ... a crime ... a crime ...

Sequence 13
DOWN WITH THE JEWS

Chorus and percussion

Original	*Translation*
A bas les juifs	**Down with the Jews**

Français, arrachons notre France	Frenchmen let us rescue France
Aux Juifs perfides et maudits.	From these accursed Jews
Jurons-le plus de tolérance	Tolerance we'll show them not
Pour cette race de bandits.	Nor give them strength anew
Pour défendre notre patrie	To save our country from their grasp
Partout formons des bataillons.	A fighting band will form
Pour terraser la Juiverie	A pride of lions we'll become
Devenons tous comme de lions.	And ban them from these shores
Pour terraser la Juiverie	A pride of lions we'll become
Devenons tous comme de lions.	And ban them from these shores
Nous gémissons dans l'esclavage	We tremble in the slavery
Des traîtres et des imposteurs,	Of traitors and of cheats
secouons le honteux servage	Save us from this servitude
de ces youpins faux et menteurs.	Imposed by lying Yids
Allons braves antisémites,	March on brave anti-Semites
Trop longtemps ils furent nos rois,	They've ruled us far too long
Leurs audaces sont sans limites	Their arrogance is limitless
Il faut reconquérir nos droits.	Our lands win back and hold.

DRUMONT Listen to the cry emanating from all the corners of France "Down with the Jews"! Certainly it is a cry from the past, but it is also a cry of the future, for whenever man suffers the same pain he utters the same cry...

ZOLA There is no deed more heroic than that of the struggle for truth and justice.
There is nothing greater or more noble.

DRUMONT The demonstrations taking place all over France to the shouts of "Down with the Jews!" are, however, very significant. They express quite clearly what the country wants.

ZOLA By which morality, by which G–d are we guided?

DRUMONT The impudence, the detestable mad impudence of this race so sure it has conquered France.

ZOLA It is anti-Semitism we have to thank for the whole of this
lamentable affair.

It was this alone which made the judicial error possible.
It is this alone, which today, drives the crowds insane.

DRUMONT Death to the Jews!

The cry was uttered at the same time, with the same force,
with the same ardour and with the same sincerity as before and, once again, without urging.

ZOLA Forbidden to speak! The shameful terror reigns, the
bravest amongst us are becoming cowards. No-one dares
to say any more what he thinks, for fear of being denounced
as a traitor.

DRUMONT I drink to the Republic, to the French Republic which
will rid you of these Jews! I drink to France, for to cry "Long
live France!" is to cry "Down with the Jews!" as France is
dying from the Jews.

Long live the Republic!
Down with the Jews!

Sequence 14
CODA

Chorus and orchestra

During the Coda, the chanteuse reads extracts from letters of Dreyfus from Devil's Island.

Violent palpitations of the heart this morning. I am suffocating. The machine struggles on. How much longer can this last? Terrible heat. The hours are like lead.

    This must end.

    Ah! Humanity.

    Ah! My beloved children.

DRUMONT *(With percussion)* The Jews have to be eternally blind as they have always been not to realise what is awaiting them. They will be taken away as scrap and the people that they oppress so harshly, that they exploit with such ferocity, will dance with joy when they learn that justice has been done.

    The leader who will suddenly emerge incarnating the idea of an entire nation will do whatever pleases him. He will have the right of life and death; he will be able to employ any means that suit his purpose.

    We will ask him to satisfy what is in the hearts of all of us, the need for justice, and to punish those who deserve it.

    The great organiser who will unite the resentments, anger and suffering, will achieve a result which will resound through the universe. He will return to Europe its prestige for 200 years.

    Who is to say that he is not already at work?

Sequence 15
FINALE

Departure of participants.

Chanteuse approaches the painter, takes the brush and begins to paint. She points to the graffiti and asks the painter.

"Is that the Dreyfus Affair?"

The painter is irritated.

"No. I'll show you what is the Dreyfus Affair!"

and kicks the bucket of paint at the wall. It is red paint. As it runs down the wall and the participants begin to depart:

ZOLA Young anti-Semites. Do they really exist? So there are young minds, young souls which have already been infected by this poison. What sorrow! What trepidation for the approaching twentieth century!

One hundred years after the Declaration of the Rights of Man, one hundred years after the supreme act of tolerance and emancipation, we are returning to the wars of religion, to the most hideous and absurd fanaticism!

And somehow we can understand this among certain men who play a role, who have an image to uphold and a voracious ambition to satisfy.

But amongst the young? Amongst those who are born and who are growing up with the blossoming of rights and freedom which we dreamt would illuminate the forthcoming century?

They are the awaited work force and are already self-declared anti-Semites. They wish to open the new century by massacring all the Jewish citizens, simply because they are of a different race and of a different faith!

The city of equality and fraternity! If our youth really came to this, we would have to weep and deny all hope for human happiness.

Oh Youth! Youth! I beg you consider the great task which awaits you. You are the architects of the future. You are the ones who will lay the foundations of the century to come which we profoundly believe will resolve the problems of the past.

Youth! Youth! Remember the suffering which your fathers endured. Those terrible battles they had to fight in order to gain the freedom in which you rejoice today.

You were not born under tyranny. You do not know what it is to awake each morning with the heel of a boot on your breast. You did not fight to escape the sword of a dictator or bear the crushing weight of a dishonest judge. Thank your fathers. Do not commit the crime of applauding lies, to campaign with brute force for the intolerance of fanatics and the greed of the ambitious. Dictatorship is the result.

Youth! Youth! Remain always on the side of justice. If the concept of justice were to fade within your soul, you will be open to grave dangers.

Youth! Youth! Be humane. Be generous. Even if we are wrong, stay with us when we say that an innocent is suffering unbearable pain and that our outraged and anguished hearts are breaking.

How can you not dream a dream of chivalry if somewhere a martyr succumbs to hatred without coming to his aid? Who, if not you, will undertake the sublime task of launching himself into this dangerous and superb cause and take the lead in the name of true justice?

Where are you heading, young people? Where are you heading you students fighting in the streets, demonstrating, casting the passions and hopes of your twenty years into the midst of our troubles?

We are heading towards humanity, truth and justice.

The lights are lowered as the participants depart but one of them returns – he has left his coat behind. He notices a swastika which has been sprayed over the painted blood – he ignores it and leaves.

END

CROSSCURRENTS

At the planning stage of *Rage and Outrage* it became clear that the artists and participants had strong views on the subject matter and its deeper meaning. It was therefore decided to film the work as a general rehearsal with the comments and responses as they occurred.

The interventions and reactions, examples of which are given here, were all spontaneous and unrehearsed.

The painter who was not aware of the details of the programme was asked to record his responses visually which he did on the rear wall of the set. Examples of his work are given herewith.

At the request of all those involved, a warning was incorporated into all the television transmissions which read as follows:

*The programme, filmed as a rehearsal,
is intended as a warning against the evils and
dangers of racism which all the participants
condemn.*

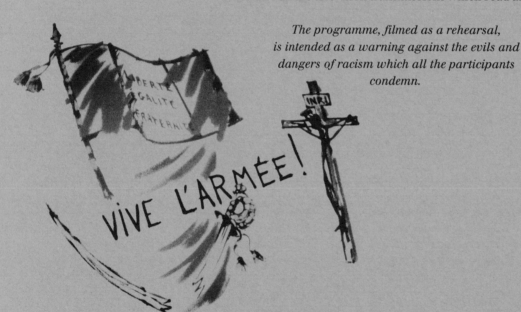

*The chanteuse Ute Lemper stops singing 'La Marseillaise Antijuive'
and is approached by the conductor Masson and the author Whyte.*

MASSON Why...
LEMPER Excuse me but I can't sing this.
WHYTE   What is the trouble?
LEMPER Excuse me, but I have an identity I have a responsibility. I don't feel like singing these words...
WHYTE   Because you have a responsibility you must sing them.
LEMPER I am not paid to sing this. There are people who will listen to it, my name is not Leni Riefenstahl or Gustaf Gründgens. I have a name and I stand for something.

WHYTE It is not a question of what you are paid for. It is a
question of humanity. I know you are suffering...

LEMPER ...and I am human.

WHYTE You are suffering, others have suffered before you.

LEMPER Excuse me, can I tell you something? Every day in
the newspapers I read in my country that there are
people who profane cemeteries, who attack immigrants'
asylums, everyday there are deaths, if there is someone,
one neo-Nazi who hears this, who likes this and who
reads this and who gives it to his pals, I am responsible
and I don't want that.

WHYTE If there is a poison of neo-Nazism....

LEMPER and I am German, excuse me...

WHYTE if there is a poison, expose it. That is your job, to
expose the poison and to destroy the poison.

MASSON Yes he is right, that's right.

LEMPER How do I know how this piece will be produced or
directed, or edited, how do I know how you are going to
use this material?

CHORUS Yes, yes...

LEMPER You think the same way, don't you?

CHORUS We have the same problem, we can't sing this.
It is loathsome. We have the same questions as you.

WHYTE We have a responsibility, we are warning, it is a
warning. Do you have children?

CHORUS Yes of course.

WHYTE There are people who no longer have children.
Where do you want your children to finish, in a
free country or do you want them to finish in a
concentration camp?

CHORUS That's a bit heavy... That's true.

WHYTE But that's life.

LEMPER It is a free country. But for the Jews it is much easier
because you know what has happened.

WHYTE It's easier? How many people did your family lose in
the war, if you tell me it's easier?

LEMPER No it is not easier to live. It is not something personal
we are discussing here.

WHYTE But it is very personal...

LEMPER But I am ashamed to say these words, because I am
German. Excuse me, I have a weight on my shoulders
which I carry wherever I work and there is prejudice
and I am another generation.

WHYTE Ute, you are a beautiful girl (*interrupted*)

CHORUS Alright, alright. We have confidence.

MASSON 1 2 3 4 let's start again.

Later in the rehearsal. Lemper completes reading extract
from Dreyfus' diary. The pianist Cohen comments:

COHEN   I do not think it is easier because one is Jewish. In any
        case it is dangerous to sing it. You were right not to sing it.
LEMPER I didn't say it was more simple.
COHEN   But that's what you said.
LEMPER What I said was that if one is Jewish, one has an
        automatic distance from a text like that, one is detached,
        because you can't feel yourself guilty, you are the victim,
        if the victim accuses it is easier. If the accused accuses,
        I am German, I am an accuser it is another thing. It is not
        easier, that is not it, but if the victim accuses it is more
        obvious.
COHEN   I could not sing it, it has nothing to do with me neces-
        sarily, it is to do with everybody.

After the end of the 'Marseillaise Antijuive'.

CHORUS How can you laugh?
MASSON *(laughing)* Because I am a Jew, so I am used to it.
CHORUS But it is poison.
MASSON No, it is so stupid, that it makes me laugh.
WHYTE *(pointing to the text of the 'Marseillaise Antijuive')* This
        is evil, what happened was evil. This was sung in 1898,
        45 years later you had Auschwitz and you had Drancy.
        They are singing it again. We have to warn that is why
        you are wonderful that you do it. We must warn the
        young people today, if we don't warn them, the poison
        will destroy society, we have to do it. Actors, musicians,
        producers, it is our job. If we had spoken out in 1930
        and 1940 the tragedy may have been averted. Speak up.
        Thank you.

CHANSONS OF THE DREYFUS AFFAIR

The Dreyfus Affair gave rise to a vast quantity of songs and verses in France (estimated at over 1000) mostly anti-Semitic and anti-Dreyfusard. Piano music, usually in the form of marches, waltzes and reveries were composed in many European countries and usually dedicated to one of the protagonists of the Dreyfusard cause.

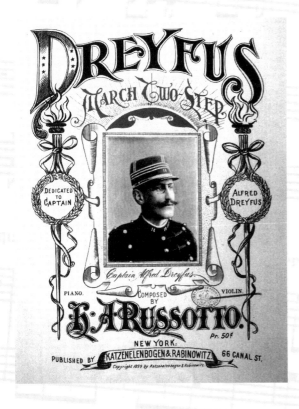

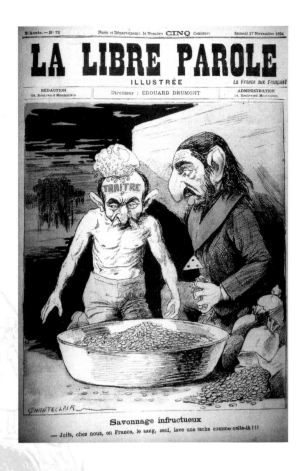

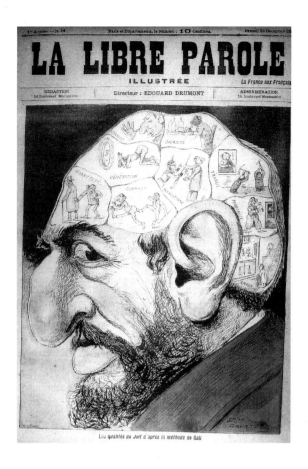

Have we not better understood the past as a
glimpse of the present, understood the wars of
religion, the leagues, the revolution, how the
peaceful masses blinded by prejudice can become
full of hate and murderers, how noble passions
such as the love of the patrie can be perverted and
misled by false ideals to the point of crime?

Gabriel Monod

Anti-Semitism…what words are there
to describe this foul disease
which would later infect a whole nation
and rationalise the massacre of millions of men,
women and children on the grounds
that Jewish blood flowed in their veins?

Pablo Casals

*...the Dreyfus Affair in its
entirety offers a foregleam
of the twentieth century...
and its anti-Semitism...*

Hannah Arendt

The Jews were first to introduce the idea of justice into the world ... All, everyone of them, my ancestors and my brothers, had the fanatical wish that everyone receive his due and that scales of the balance never be made to top unjustly. For that, for centuries now, they have shouted, sung, wept and suffered, despite the outrages, despite the insults, despite being spat upon. I am one of them and I wish to be one.

Bernard Lazare

Didn't I tell you that Captain Dreyfus belonged to a class of pariahs? He was a soldier, but he was a Jew, and it was as a Jew above all that he was prosecuted. Because he was a Jew he was arrested, because he was a Jew he was indicted, because he was a Jew he was convicted, and it is because he is a Jew that the voices of truth and justice cannot be raised on his behalf.

Bernard Lazare

The anti-Semite is, in the very depths of his heart, a criminal. What he wishes, what he prepares, is the death of the Jew.

Jean-Paul Sartre

You see
there are
four dates.
Perhaps soon
there will be
a fifth.

Ute Lemper

1834
1933
1943
199

PAS DE FAIBLESSE
PAS DE PITIÉ
POUR LES JUIFS

PAS DE FAIBLESSE
PAS DE PITIÉ
POUR LES JUIFS

1894
1933
1943
199

MY BURNING PROTEST

Paraphrase based on *La vérité en marche* by Emile Zola
Monologue for bass voice and orchestra

Zola at his trial. "Dreyfus is innocent – I swear it."

What G – d reigns over us?
What morals guide us?

Never has an assassin
Never has a man insane
been so closely guarded.
The eternal silence
the slow agony
the curse of a whole people.

A hidden poison
has led us to delirium.
Hatred for the Jew
there lies the guilt

the daily ritual
recited year in year out
in the name of morality
in the name of Christ.

This barbaric campaign
a mirror of dark ages
shatters our brotherhood
and horrifies my passion
for tolerance and justice.

What is more simple
what is more natural
than to expose the truth?

But here is the black soul
the abominable figure
the traitor
who sells his brothers
as Judas sold his G – d.

And,
if no reason is found
to explain the crime
is it enough
that he is a Jew?

Now,
dare you say
he is innocent?

Ah! when I was young
I saw
the passions of youth
its love of freedom
and hatred of force
which crushes the soul.

Now fresh minds
infected by this poison
greet a new century
declaring
they will massacre all the Jews
for they are of another race
another faith.
What horror this portends
at the dawn
of the new century.

Oh Youth! Dear Youth!
be human
be generous
strive for the cause of justice
for who will
if not you?

Youth! Dear Youth!
I beg you
think of the great task
which awaits you.

If the glow of justice
fades within you
you could fall victim
to great danger.

Youth! Dear Youth!
and you dear students
where are you heading
roaming through the streets
cleansing our discords
with the passions and hope
of your twenty years?

We are marching towards humanity
towards truth
towards justice!

France!

In these frightful days
of moral strife
when consciences darken
dear France I speak to you
to the Nation
to the Homeland.

I will dare speak all
for my passion
is the truth
and the truth is on the march
nothing will stop it.

France
how have your people
succumbed to such depths
of bigotry?
Beware
you are heading to dictatorship
to the Church of the past
with its prejudice and dogma.

France
you have allowed
the rage of hatred
to lash the face of your people

poisoned and fanatic
they scream in the streets
Down with the Jews!
Death to the Jews!

What anguish
what sadness
in the souls of those
who love you.

Dear France
I beg of you
examine your conscience
return to yourself
to the great power
you are.

France! Awake!
Think of your glory
be fair
be generous
whatever assails your reason now
you are the future
and you will awake
in the glory
of truth and justice.

President of the Republic!

A court has acquitted
one who is guilty
and spat in the face
of all truth and justice.

I will then tell the truth
as I have pledged
if the courts of justice
so empowered
do not.

It is my duty to speak
for I will not conspire
to abet a crime
My night would be haunted
by the spectre

of an innocent
his frightful torture
for a crime
he did not commit.

My President
it is to you I proclaim the truth
it is to you I turn
in revolt
and with all the force
of an honest man.

Oh the empty accusation!
To condemn a man thus
is a miracle of iniquity.
What a spectacle
what infamy
a man
weighed down with debts and crime
is proclaimed innocent
while the soul of honour
a man without stain
is dragged in the mire.
A country which has come to this
must collapse and decay.

Honest folk
I challenge you
read it and know it
your hearts will pound
with anger and revolt
when you think
of that fearful suffering
on Devil's Island
for the vanity of honoured men
who grind their boots
into the nation
stabbing its throat
as it cries out for truth
their hideous excuse
for reasons of State!
But, the truth grows
when buried underground
it gathers a force
so violent

that the day it bursts
it carries all with it.

Truth is on the march
and nothing will stop it!

President of the Republic

I accuse the Ministers of War,
the courts, the Generals
and their staff and all
who collaborated with them.

I accuse them
of being the diabolical agents
of a judicial error
and defending their deadly work
with revolting cunning.

I accuse them
of being scoundrels
and holding an inquest
of monstrous partiality.

I accuse them
of lying and of fraud
of leading a vile campaign
to mislead the public
and hide their sins.

I accuse them
of violating all human rights
by condemning a man
on testimony kept from him.

I accuse them
of concealing this illegal act
and acquitting a man
they know is guilty.

I have but one passion
a passion for light
in the name of humanity
that has suffered
and has a right

to happiness.
My burning protest
is the cry of my soul
Let them dare
and take me to the courts
let us all be tried
in the full light of day.

I am waiting.

Meeting of the council of the Légion d'honneur on the role of Zola in the Dreyfus Affair.

Public jubilation at the verdict of guilty following Zola's trial.

L'AFFAIRE ZOLA

The search warrant.

Fate and courage swept him to the summit,
to be, for one moment, the conscience of mankind.

Anatole France on Emile Zola

THE DREYFUS
AFFAIR

OPERA
IN TWO ACTS

ACT I

Courtyard of the Ecole Militaire, Paris. Cold winter morning.
Sharp wind. Occasional sun. Light snow. Troops line the square.
Assembly includes Dreyfus' fellow officers, veterans, diplomats, etc.
Outside the railings the press and a vast unruly crowd. Whistling,
booing and jeering. General Darras on horseback in the centre of
the square. Staff officers behind him.

CROWD *(Chorus)* Bloody Jew. Filthy Jew.
    Death to the traitor!
    Death to the traitor!
    (Speech Chorus) Death to the Jew, the filthy Jew, the
    traitor. Death to the filthy Jew, the traitor.
    (Chorus) Death to the traitor, death to the Jew.
    Death. Bloody Jew.

Silence descends on the square. Dreyfus appears escorted by a
sergeant-major and four gunners. He enters, tries to walk proud-
ly, stumbles and recovers. He is marched in front of General Darras
where he stands to attention. His escorts retire four paces. Darras
glares down at Dreyfus. He raises himself in his stirrups and holds
his sword high.

GENERAL DARRAS Alfred Dreyfus. You have been found guilty
    of the crime of high treason and sentenced to perpetual
    deportation and to military degradation. You are no long-
    er worthy to bear arms. In the name of the French peo-
    ple we degrade you.
DREYFUS Soldiers. An innocent man is being degraded.
    Vive la France. Vive l'Armée.
CROWD *(Speech Chorus)* Bloody Jew. Filthy Jew.
    Death to the traitor.
    Kill the bloody Jew.
    (Chorus) Bloody Jew. Filthy Jew.
    Death to the traitor.
    Death to the Jew. Death.

The giant figure of Sergeant-Major Bouxin approaches the con-
demned man. Brutally he rips the decorations from Dreyfus' cap
and sleeves, the red stripes from his trousers, his epaulettes and
all the insignia of his rank. He casts it all on the ground. He takes
Dreyfus' sabre and scabbard and shatters them over his knee.

DREYFUS I am innocent. I swear on the heads of my wife and
    children. I am innocent.

CROWD *(Speech Chorus)* Bastard. Yid. Traitor. Pig!
    (Chorus) Death to the Jew. Bastard.
    Death to the traitor.
    Death to the bloody Jew.
DREYFUS I am innocent.

Dreyfus is now a tattered figure. He is paraded in front of the troops and his fellow officers. He passes the veterans.

VETERANS *(Speech Chorus)* Silence. Bastard.
    Filthy Jew. Traitor. Dirty pig.
DREYFUS I am innocent.
    Vive la France. Vive l'Armée.
CROWD *(Speech Chorus)* Death to the traitor.
    The filthy Jew. Bastard.
    Jewish traitor.
    (Chorus) Death to the Jew. The bastard. Death to the
    traitor.
DREYFUS You have no right to insult me.
    I am innocent.
CROWD *(Speech Chorus)* Death to the traitor. Bastard! Judas!
    Filthy Yid! Boo!
    (Chorus) Bastard! Judas! Filthy Yid! Boo! Death to the
    traitor.
    Death to the traitor!
DREYFUS I am innocent. I am innocent. Innocent.
CROWD *(Speech Chorus)* Boo! Bastard. Judas.
    Beat the filthy pig to death. Traitor.
    (Chorus) Bastard. Judas. Death to the traitor.
DREYFUS Innocent…in…innocent.
CROWD *(Chorus)* Death to the Jews!
    Death to the Jews!

At the end of the courtyard two gendarmes seize Dreyfus, handcuff him and haul him into a prison van. The crowd has become hysterical. The military band strikes up the march 'Sambre et Meuse'. Cheering, howling, whistling.
    Mathieu and Lucie visit Dreyfus in prison. They do not know but it is the last time they will see him for five years. The prisoner is separated from the visitors by double bars. The prison director is always present. Mathieu and Lucie arrive and wait in the corridor. As they hear the clatter of prison keys and the doors, Lucie shudders.

LUCIE I want to kiss Alfred,
    ask if I may.

MATHIEU *(Approaching the prison director)*
    His wife would like to kiss her husband. His wife Lucie
    seeks your permission to kiss her husband.
PRISON DIRECTOR No, no. It is not allowed.
MATHIEU But just think they may be parted for ever.
PRISON DIRECTOR No!

Mathieu exits. Lucie goes up to him anxiously.

LUCIE May I?
MATHIEU No. It's not allowed.

*Lucie enters the prison area. Alfred is looking at a small photo-
graph of Lucie and his children. Dreyfus and Lucie stand silently
for a moment, lost and embarrassed in front of the prison director.*

DREYFUS A blind anger invades my heart when I think of our
    little ones suffering because of their father. What am I doing
    here? Is it an hallucination? Then I look at my tattered
    clothes and I know it is reality. Even the convicts around
    me are worth more than a traitor. At least they killed for
    jealousy or revenge. My bitterness is great. My heart is torn
    and bleeding. But I will fight until my dying breath. I only
    have one aim in life, to find the guilty one.
LUCIE Courage my darling, courage. One day you will see your
    children again. Promise me you will live. Without you I
    cannot exist. I cannot exist without you.
DREYFUS Do not weep my darling, do not weep. Fix your gaze
    ahead of you. Move the hearts of other wives and mothers.
    Cry out my innocence. Cry it, cry it from the rooftops so
    that the walls will shake. Cry it out.
LUCIE I implore you bear your torment bravely. I share your sor-
    row, the suffering and the shame. I will fight until the whole
    world recognizes your innocence.
DREYFUS I feel your heart beating so close to mine. So close, so
    close. I have loved you so deeply, always. I have loved you
    from the depths of my heart.
LUCIE/DREYFUS The thought of you and our children will
    give me strength.
LUCIE *(Approaching the prison director)* May I hold his hand?
PRISON DIRECTOR No, it is not allowed. Time is up.
DREYFUS *(Lost in his thoughts)* One day in our dear France, there
    will arise a man, honest and courageous, who will discover
    the truth. My darling, until tomorrow. Lucie, until tomor-
    row.
LUCIE My darling, until tomorrow Alfred.

They reach out to each other, but cannot touch. Lucie departs, then stops and remains standing deep in her thoughts. She overhears in the background

PRISON DIRECTOR Strip him! Search him! Clap him in irons. He leaves for Devil's Island tonight.

Lucie rushes back but the iron doors are slammed in her face. She collapses in horror in Mathieu's arms.

Night falls. Interlude. The journey to Devil's Island.

Devil's Island. Dreyfus alone in his cell. It is night. Guards outside. The Tricolore. A guard flashes a light in his face through the cell window. Dreyfus awakes with a start.

DREYFUS My brain reels and my blood burns. Fever devours me. When will all this end? Silence. Eternal silence. Never a human voice. I am alone.

In the scenes which follow, Dreyfus remembers or dreams episodes in his life. These are re-enacted on stage and, simultaneously, he reacts to his memories on Devil's Island.

> *Dreyfus falls back in his bunk. He dreams of the synagogue when he was a boy during the Franco-Prussian War. He remembers the prayers and the sound of the approaching German Army.*

CONGREGATION *(Hebrew)* Adauschem Echod.

CANTOR I Schema Yisroel Adauschem Elaukenu Adauschem Echod. Echod.

CANTOR II Schema Yisroel Adauschem Elaukenu Adauschem Echod.

CANTOR III Schema Yisroel Adauschem Echod.

RABBI Eternal God, Lord of the Universe, from your holy dwelling place bless and protect the French People. I beseech the God of Israel to imbue the Ministers of France with the spirit of goodwill for the children of Israel.

CANTOR I Ovinu Malkenu chosvenu besefer chayim tauvim. Ovinu Ovinu Malkenu batel machschwaus saunenu. Ovinu Malkenu Ovinu Ovinu Malkenu kera roah gezar dinenu.

CONGREGATION *(Bass voices)* Schema Yisroel Adauschem Elaukenu Adauschem Echod.

CANTOR II/III Echod.

RABBI In this great country of France whose flag is a glorious and immortal symbol of justice, brotherhood and liberty, we, the sons of Israel, have become equals.

LUCIE *(From afar)* Alfred is innocent, innocent, innocent.
  Vive la France. Vive l'Armée.
DREYFUS Vive la France. Vive l'Armée.
RABBI May France at this time of conflict be strong and victo-
  rious. Long live France, France and her army.
CONGREGATION Long live France, France and her army.

The voice of Dreyfus as a boy is heard.

THE BOY DREYFUS Papa, when I grow up,
  I want to be a soldier.

Dreyfus dreams of his passing out parade. Marching cadets are seen and heard.

CADETS Honour and Glory the Class of Eighty Two.
  Honour and Glory to the officer cadets.
  Liberté, Egalité, Fraternité.
  Vive la France, vive l'Armée.

The Cadets receive their accolades. So does Dreyfus.
(Fellow cadets gaze at him suspiciously.)

Dreyfus wakes from his sleep. He thinks of Lucie.

DREYFUS Lucie, my thoughts are with you. You are my strength.
  I must live. I must prove my innocence.

On one part of the stage the German Embassy in Paris comes into view. Schwartzkoppen is in his office with Esterhazy. Madame Bastian is hiding in the corridor.

ESTERHAZY The material is important. It is worth a high price.
  This 'bordereau' contains valuable information. I will be
  back with more.

Esterhazy hands the documents to Schwartzkoppen, who hands him money in return.

DREYFUS If I would only know who the guilty one is. I must find
  out. I must find out. I have to find out. I am innocent, innocent, innocent.
ESTERHAZY *(With false pathos)* It is contemptible to betray one's
  fatherland, but I have no other choice. It is for my wife and
  my children. I must save them from poverty and ruin. I
  cannot say more.

After Esterhazy leaves, Schwartzkoppen studies the 'bordereau', he tears it up and throws it into the wastepaper basket. He leaves his office. Madame Bastian empties the basket into her apron. She hands its contents to Commandant Henry, who comes to make his regular collection.

On Devil's Island, Dreyfus dreams of the intimate family atmosphere at home. He hears Lucie playing the piano. Mathieu, Pierre and Jeanne are there. The office of Mercier comes slowly into view.

DREYFUS *(Island)* My dear Pierre, my little Jeanne, darling Lucie, I love you all from the depths of my heart. I love you with all my heart. I cannot say more.

LUCIE *(At home, sings a lullaby to her children)* In the Holy Temple, in the corner, sits the mother Bat-Zion alone.

DREYFUS *(Island)* Aaaaaaaa.

MERCIER *(In his office)* This must cease. Military secrets passing into the hands of the enemy. Traitors in the Army. My career is at stake.

LUCIE *(At home)* Sits the mother Bat-Zion alone. Her two sweet children she rocks with love and sings them to sleep with a lullaby.

DREYFUS *(Island)* Aaaaaaaa.

MERCIER *(Office)* What is the bureau doing? Sleeping?

HENRY *(Office)* Minister. More evidence has come to light. It is a 'bordereau', military secrets. We have gone through the listing of officers on the general staff. We have marked the suspicious one.

LUCIE *(At home)* Under the children's cradle sits a snow-white kid.

PIERRE *(At home)* Cradle, kid.

JEANNE *(At home)* Cradle, kid.

LUCIE/PIERRE/JEANNE *(At home)* The kid, destined to wander. Will this be your fate? Raisins and almonds. Raisins ... and ... almonds. Sleep...my little ones...sleep.

DREYFUS *(Island)* Aaaaaaaa.

MERCIER *(Office)* Yes, of course, a Jew. A Jew from the Alsace, Alfred Dreyfus. Of course he is the guilty one.

HENRY *(Office)* We have compared their handwriting. Here they are.

MERCIER *(Office)* They look similar. Test his handwriting. Interrogate him. Make him confess. Prepare the order for his arrest.

LUCIE *(At home)* Sleep now, my little ones, sleep.

MERCIER *(Office)* It is to be kept secret.

(As he is leaving) Lose no time.

DREYFUS *(Island)* Aaaaaaaaaa... Cradle, kid, children, children, little ones... sleep.

Dreyfus dreams of his arrest at Army Headquarters. Present: Du Paty, Gribelin and others. Henry is behind the curtain. Du Paty wears a black glove over his right hand. Dreyfus only appears to be present.

DU PATY Complete this inspection form. I have a letter to write to the General. I have hurt my finger. Could you write it for me?
(Dictates a prepared text) Having to re-acquire the documents I passed to you before my departure on manœuvres, please return them urgently. They concern firstly a note on the hydraulic brake of the 120 Cannon.
(Du Paty interrupts his dictation) What is wrong with you Captain? You are trembling. Are your fingers cold? Be careful. This is serious.
(Continuing the dictation) Secondly, a note concerning the covering troops. Thirdly, a note on Madagascar.
(Du Paty puts his hand on Dreyfus' shoulder) Dreyfus, in the name of the law I arrest you. You are accused of high treason.
DREYFUS *(Island)* I...I...I don't understand,
I, I protest, I protest.

Du Paty picks up a copy of the penal code, revealing a revolver.

DU PATY Whoever has conspired or is in contact with the intelligence services of a foreign power shall be punished by death.
DREYFUS *(Island)* I have never had such contacts, I love my homeland, I am incapable of betrayal. I am the victim of a frightful plot.
DU PATY By death, shall be punished by death. The evidence is overwhelming. Overwhelming.

The office at headquarters is faded out.

Dreyfus feverish on the island. He remembers the scene in the prison cell after his arrest. Du Paty arrives carrying a box containing fragments of handwriting.

DREYFUS Is that box Du Paty's? Am I to identify handwritings? This is mine. This I do not know. And this? I do not know. This is mine, and this one I do not know, mine, do not know, mine, yours, his, mine, not mine, mine, not mine, mine, not mine, mine, not mine...

Dreyfus collapses. He is startled by the sound of Du Paty's voice. Dreyfus follows the orders of Du Paty on the island like a madman.

DU PATY *(Behind the stage)* Write standing up 'manœuvre'. Now sit down and write it. Write it again. Now crouch on the floor, write 'I am', hunch over the bed and write 'leaving on manœuvres'. Now put on this glove and write it, and now lie on the floor and write it.

Dreyfus remains lying on the floor (island).

DU PATY *(Backstage)* I will come at night when he is asleep. I will flash a light in his face. Perhaps he will utter a guilty phrase.

Dreyfus tries to raise himself (island).

DREYFUS My sole crime was to be born a Jew.

Dreyfus on the island remembers the military courtroom where he was tried. Large figure of Christ on the wall. Present: Seven judges (including the presiding judge) – all army officers, guards, Henry, handwriting experts and Picquart. The text of the oath is heard.

(Chorus – male voices) I swear by Almighty God, to speak the truth, the whole truth and nothing but the truth.
JUDGE Commandant Henry?
HENRY A person of honour warned me that an officer in the Ministry is a traitor.
   (He points to the imagined figure of Dreyfus in the dock.) This man is the traitor.
   (Dreyfus reacts furiously on the island) I am not naming the informer. These are military secrets.
JUDGE *(Presiding)* Do you state on your honour that the treacherous officer mentioned is Captain Dreyfus?
HENRY *(Raising his hand to the cross on the wall)* I swear it!
JUDGE Captain Alfred Dreyfus, do you have anything to say? No. Then the judges shall retire to consider their verdict.

The courtroom clears. The judges deliberate alone. During their deliberations Du Paty arrives with a secret dossier. He hands it to the judges. Du Paty withdraws. The courtroom reassembles. Each judge give his verdict as he looks at the dossier.

OFFICER Present Arms! *(A dreadful silence. All the judges raise their hands to their caps in military salute)*

JUDGE *(Presiding)* In the name of the French people!

Is Alfred Dreyfus, Captain in the Artillery, guilty of having dealings with a foreign power to the detriment of the nation?

JUDGES I – VII *(Individually)*

Guilty! Guilty! Guilty! Guilty! Guilty! Guilty! Guilty!

JUDGES *(Together)* Guilty!

DREYFUS *(Remembers the degradation with horror)*

Innocent man degraded.

(He hears the insults of the crowd)

CROWD Dreyfus, hahaha, hahaha, Captain, guilty, haha.

Death to the traitor. Death to the Jews.

Filthy Jew. Bloody Jew. Death to the traitor.

Lucie alone in her temporary home. Three years have passed. In her desperation she addresses a supplication to the Pope.

LUCIE Holy ... Holy Father! I, Lucie Dreyfus, prostrate at the feet of your Holiness, most humbly supplicate the mercy and compassion of the father of the Catholic Church. I declare that my husband Alfred, Captain in the French Army and of Jewish descent, is innocent, innocent. He is the victim of a judicial error. As he is severed from all contact with humankind, this petition is signed by his grief-stricken wife, who in tears looks towards the Vicar of Christ, as formerly the daughter of Jerusalem turned to Christ himself.

Lucie is joined by Pierre, Jeanne and friends, amongst them Zola.

LUCIE Monsieur Zola, I have told you everything. We are desperate. Three years have passed. We are at the bottom of an abyss. I have even addressed a petition to his Holiness the Pope. If we do not find the truth, if he dies there, what will happen to his children?

ZOLA Madame, I feel your anguish.

MATHIEU *(Enters, excited)* Monsieur Zola, although I am watched, followed and threatened, I have distributed several thousand copies of the 'bordereau' throughout Paris, in the hope that someone will recognise the handwriting, but nothing. At long last a banker has recognised the handwriting of one of his clients. It is that of Count Ferdinand Walsin Esterhazy, a major in the infantry. I must pass this information immediately to the Ministry of War. *(Mathieu leaves)*

ZOLA The truth is on the march, the truth, the truth. I feel a great
       injustice has been committed, I will support your cause.

*Lucie, Pierre, Jeanne and friends are faded away. Concentration
on Zola.*

ZOLA What is more simple, what is more natural, than to expose
       the truth?
       (He becomes lost in his thoughts) Honest folk, I challenge
       you, read it and know it. Your hearts will pound with anger
       and revolt when you think of that fearful suffering on
       Devil's Island. It is my duty to speak as I will not conspire
       to abet a crime. My nights would be haunted by the spec-
       tre of an innocent, his frightful torture for a crime he did
       not commit. A hidden poison has led us to delirium. Hatred
       of the Jews. There lies the guilt. The daily ritual, recited
       year in year out, in the name of morality, in the name of
       Christ. Now fresh minds, infected by this poison, greet a
       new century declaring they will massacre all the Jews, for
       they are of another race, another faith.

*The office of General Gonse. Present: Boisdeffre, Henry, Du Paty
and Gribelin. Picquart is facing the General. He carries a batch of
documents.*

PICQUART My investigations show that the court martial made
           a mistake.
ZOLA *(His voice)* ... next century ...
PICQUART I have copies of Esterhazy's handwriting and have
           compared them with the 'bordereau'. They are identical.
ZOLA *(Voice)* ... Jews ... massacred ...
PICQUART Esterhazy should be brought to his office to give an
           explanation about the 'bordereau'.
ZOLA ... from a different race ... of another faith ... another ...
       another.
GONSE Out of the question Picquart. You are lacking in balance
        in this matter.
        (Friendly) Why are you so interested in establishing the
        innocence of Dreyfus? What is it to you, if this Jew is on
        Devil's Island?
PICQUART But if he is innocent?
GONSE If you say nothing, no one will know.
PICQUART My General, what you say is despicable. The evidence
           against Esterhazy is clear. And as for this secret dossier
           (throws the dossier on the table) it contains not one piece
           of evidence against Dreyfus.

GONSE Picquart, you are only concerned with your obsession. You are neglecting your duties. You are too preoccupied. I will remove you from your post and send you to the Tunisian front.

PICQUART I do not know what I am going to do, but I will not take this secret to the grave with me. *(He picks up his papers and the secret dossier. He begins to leave. Boisdeffre beckons to Henry to retrieve the documents from him)*

HENRY Colonel, the General wishes you to leave the dossier and all other papers here. *(Picquart returns to his office)*

*The following four scenes are simultaneous. Gonse in his office **(a)** with others and later with Mercier; Du Paty in his office **(b)** with Gribelin; Picquart alone in his office **(c)**; Henry alone in his office **(d)**. Later Dreyfus on Devil's Island. The action and texts overlap.*

GONSE *(To Du Paty and Gribelin in **(a)**)* You must warn Esterhazy of Du Paty's enquiries. But he must not know that the warning comes from us. *(Du Paty returns to his office with Gribelin)*

GONSE *(To Henry in **(a)**)* We need new evidence. We need decisive evidence. Evidence which implicates Dreyfus beyond any doubt.

DU PATY *(To Gribelin in **(b)**)* We will send Esterhazy an anonymous letter to warn him. We will sign it 'Espérance'. Then I want you to visit him.

HENRY *(To Gonse in **(a)**)* If I may advise, Picquart should be removed from Paris as quickly as possible.

GONSE *(To Henry in **(a)**)* I intend to name you Chief of the Department when I have re-posted him. *(Henry leaves office **(a)** and enters office **(d)**.)*

PICQUART *(Alone in his office in **(c)**)* Fate has chosen me to discover the truth.

GRIBELIN *(In **(b)**)* Where do I find Esterhazy?

*Henry is in his office **(d)** alone. He is falsifying documents, exchanging signatures, re-arranging and re-gluing words in different ways.*

PICQUART *(in **(c)**)* An innocent trembles in jail.

DU PATY *(in **(b)**)* He keeps a whore in Rue Douai. Her name is Madame Pays. He is usually there.

PICQUART *(in **(c)**)* The traitor is walking free.

HENRY *(in **(d)** Looks at forgery. He is pleased)* Good ... very good ... I must congratulate myself.

DREYFUS *(Island)* Suffocation.

DU PATY *(in (b))* The secret meeting should be at Parc
  Monsouri, at the public urinals.

DREYFUS *(Island)* ... Air ...

HENRY *(in (d))* Really masterly.

PICQUART *(in (c))* What may have been an error, could
  become a crime.

DREYFUS *(Island)* It is unbearably hot.

BOISDEFFRE *(To Gonse in (a))* Contact General Mercier
  immediately and ask him to come here.

HENRY *(in (d))* Good ... very good. This should be sufficient.

BOISDEFFRE *(in (a))* He must inspect the secret dossier.

DREYFUS *(Island)* Fever ...

PICQUART *(in (c))* A crime, what a tragedy for France, for
  France, for France.

Mercier arrives in office (a), he is furious. He takes the secret dossier from Gonse, opens it and begins to search. He pulls out a document, lights a match and burns it.

DREYFUS *(Island)* Delirium ...

Mercier leaves (a). Gonse puts the dossier in his desk. Henry enters and hands him his forgery. Gonse studies it. He inserts it into the secret dossier which he then hands to Henry. Light goes out in the office.

Dreyfus in his cell on Devil's Island. In one hand he holds his family photograph. He kisses it. He is almost unrecognisable, a pathetic figure disintegrating physically and spiritually. His ankles are bandaged with bleeding rags. His small window has been mostly boarded up. Temperature and humidity are unbearable. Mosquitos and insects infect his cell. He fears his end is near. He stands by the window gasping for air.

DREYFUS *(Island)* ... Trembling ... strange images ... delirium.
  It is too much. It cannot last much longer. I am so weary,
  everything is black. My heart is overwrought, my heart, my
  heart, my brain is destroyed. I cannot gather my thoughts
  ... my my ... I cannot my thou ... thoughts ... not ... gather
  ... together ... Lucie my darling ... my beloved children ...
  oh I love you all, all. Love ... torture ... fever ... torment ...
  love ... anger ... aah ...

Jailers enter carrying irons. They shackle Dreyfus to his bed. Dreyfus falls into an hallucinatory state. He sees himself in his coffin, immobile (as in the cell). The Cross at the court-martial becomes visible on which he sees himself crucified. Standing by the Cross is a general (Mercier, but unrecognised by Dreyfus) drawing a sword (degradation).

ESTERHAZY *(Not recognisable, voice distorted)*
    Haha hahaha haha ...

Lucie, Mathieu, Pierre and Jeanne are on stage. They are in a maze. Dreyfus stretches his arms towards Lucie (parting) but can not reach her. The generals arrive (trial and degradation). Dreyfus beckons for their help, but they ignore him. Lucie is now running, when she finally reaches the iron gates they slam in front of her (parting).

ESTERHAZY Hahahaha haha hahaha ...
    (His satirical laughter is drowned by the orchestra)

DREYFUS ON DEVIL'S ISLAND

Devil's Island, the smallest of a group of three volcanic islands of French Guiana, served to isolate deportees and lepers, one fourth of whom died each year in the hot and unhealthy climate.

LOCATION

Devil's Island is the smallest of three islands of the Salut Archipelago situated off the fever stricken and swampy coast of French Guiana just north of the equator. The barren island is 400 metres wide and 1200 metres long and is surrounded by shark infested waters. The climate is harrowing with extremes of temperature and humidity. Malaria, disease and death were often the fate of the deportees. Dreyfus was to be the only prisoner there, imprisoned and held in solitary confinement under constant surveillance.

Dreyfus arrived on Devil's Island and was locked into his prison cell on the afternoon of 14 April 1895. On the same day he commenced a diary, intended for his wife Lucie: *"Today, I begin the diary of my sad and tragic life."* And the same night: *"It is impossible for me to sleep. This cage in front of which the guard walks up and down like a phantom appearing in my dreams, the plague of insects which run over my skin, the rage which is smothered in my heart that I should be here... When shall I again pass a calm and tranquil night? Perhaps not until I find*

in the tomb the sleep that is everlasting." And later still in the night: *"Where are the beautiful dreams of my youth and the aspirations of my manhood? My heart is dead within me; my brain reels with the turmoil of my thoughts. What is the mystery underlying this tragedy? Even now I understand nothing of what has passed."*

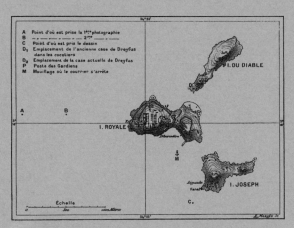

Map of the Iles du Salut.

CONDITIONS OF DETENTION

His iron cage was a stone hut with iron gratings on the two small windows. The door a lattice work of iron bars. A guard, stationed at the entrance, was changed every two hours. A large observation tower was constructed, about 50 feet high – the Mirador – with a guard constantly on duty. The tower was armed with a Hotchkiss gun.

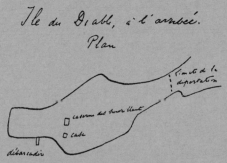

Captain Dreyfus' sketch of Devil's Island.
The difficulty of access to Devil's Island constituted
a guarantee against any attempt to approach the
area of imprisonment of the deportee.

In an ever more depraved circle of cruelty and paranoia, the conditions of imprisonment were made more punitive. The prisoner was transferred twice to a newly constructed and "more secure" complex; the number of guards increased from 5 to 15; the tiny windows were raised and a palisade constructed which blocked out any view; additional covers on the windows brought the prisoner to the point of suffocation; the cell was lit at night and the constant gaze of his guards "never allowed to let him out of their sight", was pitiless humiliation. Conversation was forbidden. "A tomb had closed in on the prisoner", and in the words of his brother Mathieu "every passing hour was a century of suffering and another step towards death".

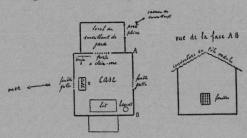

Plan of the prison hut. Drawing by Dreyfus.

The prisoner's condition soon began to deteriorate. Repeated bouts of high fever, increasingly frequent losses of consciousness, a sensation of wasting away, his body stooped and bent, the face hollow and jaundiced, his beard prematurely white, his head balding. One night he fell unconscious from his bed and was found inanimate and covered in blood. His every instance was a fight against the loss of his reason and every evening after mustering all his energy to silence the palpitation of his heart, he sank into a terrible depression.

Joseph Reinach, Histoire de L'Affaire Dreyfus

On Sunday, 6 September 1896, Alfred Dreyfus was put in irons.

The double irons consisted of two shackles in the form of a U joined to a metal stem which was fastened to the bed. When applied, the body was forced into complete rigidity.

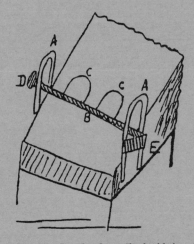

Sketch by Dreyfus. Irons "la double boucle" with
which Dreyfus was shackled to his bed at night.

Riveted to his bed by chains stained with blood, tortured by vermin and torrid heat, racked by spiritual torment, Dreyfus felt that his suffering had passed the limits of human endurance and that he should die. He had difficulties gathering his thoughts and began to write and sketch the same motives over and over again.

van de Schakspeare tan Othello — [illegible] + 3

Who steals my purse, steals trash, 'tis something, nothing —
'Twas mine, 'tis his, and has been slave to thousands
But he that filches from me my good name
Robs me of what which not enriches him
And makes me poor indeed. —

Page from Dreyfus' diary with quotation from Othello.

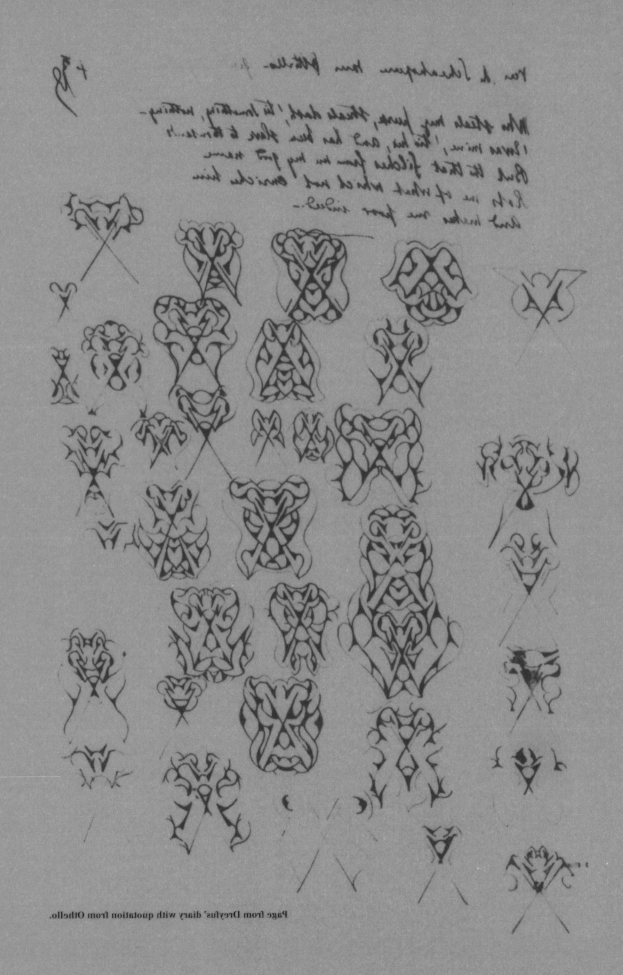

Othello III, 5
Who steals my purse steals trash,
  'tis something nothing,
'Twas mine, 'tis his, and has been
  slave to thousands,
But he that filches from me my good name
Robs me of that which not enriches him,
And makes me poor indeed.

Alfred Dreyfus spent 1614 days and nights incarcerated on Devil's Island. His survival was a feat of extraordinary stoicism and a bitter blow to his oppressors.

Medical report given by Dr. Veugmon the physician who had Dreyfus in his charge while he was prisoner on Devil's Island:

Dreyfus is a neuropathic subject, and the regime to which he has been subjected has made him more so; isolation, idleness, boredom, and discouragement irritate his nervous system. His malady displayed itself about a year after his imprisonment had commenced, and took the form of cerebral depression. He was beset by unconquerable sadness.

In my presence Dreyfus was always self-possessed. Under his strength of will one could detect, however, stormy symptoms, and his jailers said that often, when first awakening of a morning, he would break out into expressions of fury, bursting into tears, gesticulating wildly and shouting unintelligible words. These violent rages usually resulted in utter exhaustion and general torpor, and sometimes in syncope, when, of course, I was sent for.
Rapport officiel at the Rennes Trial

The prison hut of Dreyfus drawn by a warder.

מגילת דרייפוס

דרייפוסעס מאטערניש

בעקאַנטליך איז דרייפוס
געווען איינגעשפּאַרט אין אַ קליין הילצערנעם הייזעל אויף דער
טייפעלס אינזעל. ווען קאָלאָנעל פּיקאַרד האָט אין יאָהר 1896
מיטגעטהיילט דעם גענעראַל בילאָט, אַז דרייפוס איז אונשולדיג,
האָט מען דרייפוסעס הייזעל אומרינגעלט מיט אַ הילצערנעם
צוים. דיזער אַקט איז געווען אין גאַנצען גאָר אינגעזעצליך,
דען דרייפוס איז נור געוואָרען פעראורטהיילט צו לעבענס-
לענגליכע פערבאַנונג אין אַ בעפעסטיגען פּלאַבין. עס זיינען
אבער נאָך אנדערע זאַכען דאָ, וואָס דיא פראַנצויזען מוזען וויסען:
מען וואָלט געגלויבט אַז דער צוים אַרום דרייפוסעס היי-
זעל, וואָלט געווען אַזוי ווייט ער זאָלל ווייניגסטענס קענען רע-
ניסען דיא פרישע לופט אָדער זעהען דעם הימעל, דאָס איז
אבער ניט געווען געווען דער פאַלל. דער צוים איז אבער געווען אַזוי
נאַהענט צום הייזעל אױפגעשטעלט אַז עס איז נור געווען 16
צאָלל רוום צווישען דעם הייזעל און דעם צוים. נון שטעלט
אייך פאָר, וואָס דאָס. בערייטעט 16 צאָלל, עס איז קוים עט-
וואָס מעהר ווא אַ פוס. דיא טראָפּישע לופט אויף דער טיי-
פּעלס אינזעל איז סיא ווא סיא. סיא. שוויל און דריקענד, מען האָט
דיא גרעסטע מיהע צו אטהעמען, אפילו אין דער פרייער לופט.
ווען מען האָט דעם צוים אַזוי נאָהנם געשטעלט צום הייזעל,
האָט מען דיא ביסעל פרייע לופט און ליכט אין גאַנצען אַוועק
גענומען פון דרייפוס. דער אָרעמער געפיינגטער איז כמעט
געוואָרען דערשטיקט און דער דאָקטאָר. האָט פערלאַנגט מען
זאָל דרייפוס'ן מעהר לופט געבען. גלויבט איהר אַז מען האָט
ערווייטערט דעם רוב צווישען דעם צוים און דעם הייזעל ?
ניט אים מינדעסטענס. מען האָט נור דעם דאַך פון היים
אַ ביסעל העכער געמאַכם. וואָס אַנבעטרעפּט דיא אייזערנע
רינגען, וואָס דרייפוס האָט געהאט, זאָ זיינען זיא געווען אוא
באַרב, ווא מען בענוצב זייא פאר דיא ערגסטע פאַלעריען
פערברעבער. דיא רינגען זיינען געווען "דאָפּעלבע רינגען"
דאָס הייסט צו ערשט זיינען איהב דיא פים געוואָרען אַרום גע-
רינגעלב, דאן האָט מען איהם דיא האנדגעלייננגען מיט רינגען
בעלעגב דאן זיינען איהב דיא העגד און פים געוואָרען צוואַמען
געשמידב דורך קורצע אבער שווערע קעטטען. דרייפוס איז
דאהער ניב געווען אים שטאַנד צו ריהרען ניט דיא הענד אוי
ניב דיא פים. נון קען מען זיך פאָרשטעללען, וואָס דער געפיי-
ניגטער האָב געמוזט ליידען אין אַ קלימאט, וואָס דיא. לופט
איז פול מיב גיפטיגע אינזעקטען און געגען וועלכע דרייפוס
האָב זיך אפילו ניב געקאָנב אבווערהרען. אזאַ בעהאַנדלונג
געבב מען נור דיא נעסטיגסטע פערברעבער וועלכע בונםעמיען
איינער אינער, איינאַנדער.

Dreyfus was locked in a small wooden hut on
Devil's Island. When in 1895 Colonel Picquart
informed General Billot that Dreyfus was innocent,
Dreyfus' hut was surrounded with a wooden palisade. This act was absolutely illegal, for Dreyfus
had only been sentenced to life-long banishment
in a fortified place. There is still more that Frenchmen must know: One would have thought that the
palisade around Dreyfus' hut would be far enough
for him at least to be able to enjoy the fresh air or
to see the sky. But this was not the case. The palisade was so close to the hut that there was only 16
inches of space between the pallisade and the hut.
Imagine what this means! 16 inches! It is hardly
more than a foot. The tropical air on Devil's Island
is anyway stifling and oppresive, it is an effort to
breathe, even in the open air. When the palisade
was erected so close to the hut, even that little bit
of free air and light was denied to Dreyfus. The
poor sufferer was almost suffocated and the doc-
tor requested Dreyfus to be given more air. Did they
widen the space between the palisade and the
hut? Not in the least. They only slightly raised the
roof of the hut.

Regarding the iron rings applied to Dreyfus, they
were of the type used for the worst criminals. The
rings were 'double rings', that is, first his feet were
encircled, then they put rings round his wrists, then
his hands and feet were connected with short but
heavy chains. Dreyfus was therefore unable to
move either his hands or his feet. Can you imagine
what the victim had to suffer in a climate where
the air is full of poisonous insects against which
Dreyfus was not even able to defend himself. This
kind of treatment is only for the most ferocious
criminals who brawl among each other.

Extract from PEE PEE FOX (July 1899), an Anglo/American
Yiddish language periodical which serialised the plight of
Dreyfus in the form of a 'Dreyfus Megillah' (a Jewish histori-
cal scroll).

On Thursday 10 September 1896, he ends his diary with the following entry:

I am so utterly weary, so broken down in body and soul, that today I stop my diary, not being able to foresee how long my strength will hold out, or what day my brain will succumb under the weight of so great a burden. I finish it by addressing to the President of the Republic this supreme appeal, in case strength and sanity fail before the end of this horrible tragedy:

Monsieur le Président de la République:

I take the liberty of asking you that this diary, written day by day, be handed to my wife.

There will be found in it, perhaps, Monsieur le Président, cries of anger, of affright, at the most awful condemnation that ever befell a human being – a human being who never forfeited his honour. I no longer feel the courage to re-read it, to retrace the bitter journey.

Today I have no recriminations to make against anyone; each one has thought himself in the fullness of right and conscience.

I simply declare once more that I am innocent of this abominable crime, and I ask ever and again for this one thing, always the same thing – that the search for the culprit who is the real author of this base crime be diligently prosecuted.

And when he is discovered, I beseach that the compassion which so great a misfortune as mine inspires may be given to my dear wife and my darling children.

End of the Diary.

Head-warder's signature to last leaf of the diary.

The Watch Tower.

ACT II

Gaiety and revelry in the Moulin Rouge. Gambling room and chambre privée. An enormous crowd with celebrities, officers, etc. Music and dancing. A wild Can-Can is in progress. Marguerite (Marie) Pays, Esterhazy's mistress and former prostitute, moves amongst the crowd and approaches the stage. She is attractive and flirtatious.

CROWD *(Chorus I)* We want Marie. Marie give us a song!
  (Chorus II) We want Marie, a soldier's song!
MARIE I was sad and I was lonely
  nameless men took pleasure from me
  When passions rose, their pockets jingled
  when passions waned, their handouts dwindled.
CROWD Poor Marie. Poor Marie.
  When passions waned, their handouts dwindled.
MARIE Then, one day, the bugle sounded
  and, in one fell swoop, he mounted
  sabre held high in his hand.
CROWD Bravo Marie. Bravo Marie
  Sabre held high in his hand.
MARIE If you want a gallant escort
  find a soldier, find a soldier
  If you want to thrill and gamble
  take a soldier, take a soldier
  If you want your flesh to tremble
  tremble, tremble, tremble, tremble
  ...k a soldier, ...k a soldier.
CROWD *(Chorus)* Vive Marie! Vive l'Amour! Vive l'Armée!

Esterhazy enters, a popular figure. He is cheered by the crowd. Henry is present.

CROWD *(Speech chorus I)* Long live Esterhazy.
  Three cheers Hip-Hip-Hurrah.
  (Speech chorus II) Long live Esterhazy.
  Three cheers Hip-Hip-Hurrah.
  (Chorus) Welcome. We honour you.
  We rejoice at your presence.

Henry goes to Esterhazy and greets him. Mathieu and Picquart enter. Esterhazy looks around.

ESTERHAZY *(To Henry)* You see, those bastards
  are following me.

Mathieu observes Esterhazy. Picquart instructs two of his secret serviceman to watch him.

MARIE Welcome to our hero!
        (Goes to Esterhazy and whispers in his ear)
        I want to celebrate tonight in our special way.
ESTERHAZY *(Smacking her on the bottom)* You irresistible
        wench! First I will gamble and try my luck. I need mo-
        ney. I am not as rich as they are.
        (Looking in the direction of Mathieu) Send him two old
        troopers. Perhaps they'll give him something he'll
        remember!

Two of the girls make their way to Mathieu and begin to flirt. Ester-hazy goes into the private gaming room. More and more noise as his losses grow and his temper gets worse. Marie stays outside. She flirts and moves amongst the crowd to centre stage.

MARIE Beloved guests, glorious soldiers, I present you with a
        new number which will be the rage of Paris. The Yid's
        Polka.

A group of dancers perform caricatures of Jews, Dreyfus with a long nose and a matching partner (a dancer or Marie).

MARIE V'la qu'dans les rues d'Paris
        on n'trouve plus qu'des youdis.
        A chaque pas sur votre chemin
        Vous n'voyez qu'des youpins.
        C'est une race de vermine,
        Ils ont de tristes mines.
        On d'vrait les expulser
        Ou bien les assomer.
ZOLA France, how have your people succumbed
        to such depths of prejudice?
MARIE Trala la la la
        lala la la la
        Chassez ces coquins
        Oh! les sales youpins
CROWD *(Chorus)* Trala la la la
        lala la la la
        Chassez ces coquins
        Oh! les sales youpins
ESTERHAZY *(From the gaming room)* I need money to pay.
        Give me time to pay.

MARIE D'après leur renseignements
      Dreyfus est innocent,
      Mais ils sont incapables
      D'découvrir le coupable.
      On peut l'dire sans vergogne
      Ils ont triste besogne,
      Quand leur race périra
      Alors chacun chantera
ZOLA You have... you... you have allowed the rage of hatred...
MARIE Trala la la la
      lala la la la
      Chassez les coquins
      Oh! les sales youpins
CROWD Trala la la la
      lala la la la
      Chassez ces coquins
      Oh! les sales youpins

The crowd becomes hysterical and begins to dance. People make anti-Semitic gestures. Esterhazy comes out of the gaming room. Marie goes up to him, but he pushes her aside. She caresses him. She leads Esterhazy into the chambre privée. She manœuvres him to the divan and leans over him coquettishly.

MARIE You are always running off to work, you never have
      time for me.
      (Sexily) Tell me my dear Count, what can I do for you
      tonight?
      (They begin to embrace. She sits up) Ah! There was a
      letter for you at home.
ESTERHAZY Who is it from?
MARIE *(Taking the envelope from her décolleté and looking at
      it)* There is no sender.
ESTERHAZY Come here and read it to me.
      (Esterhazy fondles her)
MARIE *(Reading)* Personal to Major Esterhazy. Your name will
      be the object of a great scandal. The Dreyfus family are
      planning to trap you. Major Picquart has bought samples
      of your handwriting and is passing documents to the family.
      They will ask for a re-trial. They will ruin you.
ESTERHAZY *(Jumping up in panic)* I must flee. Where is the train
      timetable? No, I must see Schwartzkoppen. He must save
      me. *(He paces up and down, then slumps into a chair. He
      takes a phial from his pocket)* I will kill myself.
MARIE *(Taking the phial from him)* You miserable coward. If
      you run and desert me, I'll tell everything.

ESTERHAZY *(Falling on his knees)* No, no! Swear that you will not tell, nothing, please nothing.

MARIE A man in dark glasses called today. He said it was important. You are to meet him at five tomorrow in secret in the urinals at Parc Monsouri. *(She gives him a slip of paper)*

In Parc Monsouri. The disguised Du Paty reaches out from the urinals and beckons Esterhazy to follow him.

DU PATY Do you know why we are here?

ESTERHAZY I think so. But I do not know who you are. I am the victim of a frightful plot.

DU PATY *(Theatrically)* We know of the plot against you. But do not worry, you have powerful protectors.

ESTERHAZY *(With a superior air)* I will not allow my name to be dragged through the mud. An Esterhazy fears nothing and no one. My honour is beyond reproach. I have always acted on orders.

DU PATY You must obey our instructions. Exercise caution! *(He leaves)*

Esterhazy leaves and begins to walk home. Henry arrives.

ESTERHAZY I tell you we are swimming in shit, but it is not my arse that did it. I only acted on orders.

HENRY We must clear your name.

ESTERHAZY How?

HENRY You must ask for a court-martial.

ESTERHAZY But...

HENRY You will be acquitted. *(Cheerfully)* Sabre in hand, we are going to charge.

HENRY/ESTERHAZY Sabre in hand, we are going to charge, we are going to charge. Sabre in hand, sabre in hand, we are going to charge.

They become euphoric and sing as they leave.

The street outside the courtroom where the court-martial of Esterhazy is being held. Street musicians are playing. A great crowd is gathering to hear the verdict. Drumont and his anti-Dreyfusard followers are present as well as a monk and Marie. Zola is there with his Dreyfusard friends. A rabbi and his family look on. The 'Ligue Antisemitique' and the newspaper 'La Croix' have erected stands for speakers. Violence is in the air.

STREET VENDOR I List of Jews for sale, of Jews in French
  cities. List of Jews, lists...

Drumont mounts the stand.

STREET VENDOR II Anti-Jewish songs,
  Anti-Dreyfus songs, the latest hits.
SPECTATOR Silence! Silence for the Pope of Anti-Semitism.
DRUMONT Poor Esterhazy!
CROWD *(Chorus)* Vive Esterhazy! Down with Picquart!
  Down with Picquart! Vive Esterhazy!
DRUMONT Judas sold the compassion of Christ. Dreyfus sold
  our nation.
CROWD *(Chorus)* Between the Jews and us, there stands the
  patrie.

*The monk approaches and stands next to Drumont. They compete
with each other in the following tirade.*

DRUMONT The Semite is money grabbing, greedy and sly.
MONK The Aryan is heroic, honest and naive.
DRUMONT The Semite cannot see beyond his life on earth.
MONK The Aryan lives with lofty thoughts of the ideal.
DRUMONT The Semite is a trader and deceives his
  fellow man.
MONK The Aryan is a poet, a monk and a soldier.
DRUMONT The Semite exploits the Aryan, he lives like a para-
  site in a civilisation which he did not create.
MONK ...which he did not create.
ZOLA *(Unable to control himself)* And they are your creation!
  Persecuted without a homeland, thrown into ghettos like
  lepers.
CROWD *(Chorus)* Down with Zola! Down with his syndicate.
  Let us smash Jewish power and boot them out of France.

*The crowd becomes violent and begins to stone the rabbi and his
family. The anger of the Dreyfusards has been ignited. Zola stands
up.*

ZOLA France, oh France, your people are poisoned and fanatic.
  Your people scream in the streets: "Down with the Jews.
  Death to the Jews" ... What anguish, what sadness in the
  souls of those who love you. Dear France, examine your
  conscience. Return to yourself, to the great power that you
  are. Awake in the glory of truth and justice.

Marie winds her way charmingly towards Zola. She begins almost teasingly to sing her anti-Zola song.

MARIE Quand donc finiras-tu, dis?
      Zola d'défendr' les Youdis:
      Si tu n'veux plus qu'on t'emboîte,
      Ferm' ta boîte!
      Tu n' s'ras pas d' l'Académie
      Maint'nant, c'est bien entendu,
      Finis donc ta comédie:
      T'as assez vendu!
      T'as assez vendu!

She sticks her bottom out at Zola.

CROWD *(Chorus)* Ferm' ta boîte!
      Ferm' ta boîte!
      T'as assez vendu!
MARIE Maint'nant qu' t'es rich' comm' Crésus
      N' viens pas la faire au Jésus:
      Ne prêch' pas d' ta voix benoîte;
      Ferm' ta boîte!
      De l'innocence de ton traître
      Tu restes l' seul convaincu;
      Au fond t'en rigol's peut-être;
      T'as assez vendu!
CROWD *(Chorus)* Ferm' ta boîte! Ferm' ta boîte!
      T'as assez vendu! Assez vendu!
SPECTATOR *(From the courtroom)* Quiet! Silence, the verdict!
JUDGE *(Heard from the courtroom)* In the name of the French
      people! The Supreme Court-Martial of the Military Gov-
      ernment of Paris declares unanimously, that Major Walsin
      Esterhazy is Not Guilty.
CROWD *(Chorus)* Vive Esterhazy! Vive l'Armée!

People begin to exit from the courtroom. Esterhazy appears.

CROWD *(Chorus)* Vive Esterhazy, the martyr of the Jews!
      Long live Esterhazy.

Esterhazy is congratulated. Marie kisses him. Mathieu and Picquart come out of the courtroom.

CROWD *(Chorus)* Down with Zola! Down with Picquart!
      Down, down, down with them both, down with Zola
      and Picquart!

The crowd begins to stone Mathieu, Picquart and Zola. Picquart is arrested. Zola begins to assert his authority.

ZOLA J'Accuse, J'Accuse, J'Accuse.

As Zola dominates the stage, the crowd fades away dispersing into the darkness.

ZOLA I accuse the Ministers of War, the courts, the generals and all who collaborated with them. I accuse them, I accuse them of being the diabolical agents of a judicial error and defending their deadly work with revolting cunning. I accuse them, I accuse them, I accuse them of being scoundrels and holding an enquiry of monstrous partiality. I have but one passion, a passion for life, in the name of humanity that has suffered and has a right to happiness. My burning protest is the cry of my soul.

The boulevards. Street musicians. More and more people come on stage. Open conflicts, shouting of anti-Semitic slogans, stoning and breaking of shops. An anti-Semitic army assembles carrying clubs, iron bars, etc. They burn an effigy of Dreyfus and sing the anti-Jewish Marseillaise.

CROWD *(Chorus)* Tremblez, youpins, et vous, perfides,
Le jour de gloire et arrivé.
Contre nous de la juiverie
Le troupeau hurlant s'est levé.
Le troupeau hurlant s'est levé.
Les voyez-vous dans notre France
Ces insulteurs de nos soldats.
Grossis de voyous, de rastas
Nous narguer de leur insolence.
Aux armes antijuifs, formez vos bataillons
Marchons, marchons
Qu'un sang impur abreuve nos sillons.

The crowd follows the anti-Semitic marchers.

The office of the new Minister of War Cavaignac slowly becomes visible. Present are Boisdeffre, Gonse and others. The minister sits at his desk. They are examining Henry's forgery. Zola's voice is heard from afar.

ZOLA J'Accuse! J'Accuse!

Henry enters. The Minister beckons to him.

MINISTER Did you forge a letter?
HENRY No, I did not.
MINISTER Then what did you do?
HENRY I just arranged some sentences.
MINISTER No, you forged a whole letter.
    Confess it.
HENRY I swear I did not.
MINISTER Tell us the whole truth. Confess it.
HENRY I just added some words.
MINISTER Which words? Tell me.
HENRY Words, which had nothing to do with this matter.
MINISTER You received a letter. You discarded its text and
    added another.
HENRY *(Discredited)* Yes.
    (As he is led out) I have always done my duty. I would do
    it again. It was for the good of the army. I am doomed.
    They are abandoning me.
BOISDEFFRE Monsieur le Ministre, I do not feel well.
GONSE Monsieur le Ministre, I do not feel well.
BOISDEFFRE/GONSE We have the honour of asking you to
    accept our resignation. Vive la France. Vive l'Armée.
    Glory to France.
SOLDIER *(Rushing into the room)* Henry is dead! He has
    committed suicide.

*The office of Cavaignac fades away. Lucie dominates the stage
and petitions the Supreme Court of Appeal.*

LUCIE Slowly and painfully light has been shed on a denial of
    justice. The truth has emerged. It only remains to proclaim
    it. From the depth of human pain and with eyes that have
    no more tears to shed, I turn to you, for this act of final
    justice. I await it, as a glittering testimony to your high and
    impartial justice. I await it, as a word of deliverance for
    this loyal soldier who, hounded to his prison cell by im-
    placable hatred, has submitted to his torture without
    weakness. I await it, as a breath of life for my failing heart
    so crushed by the savage anger which surrounds it.
MATHIEU *(Arriving)* The verdict has been annulled. There
    will be fresh proceedings against Alfred. The trial will be
    held in Rennes. *(He leaves)*
LUCIE *(Ecstatically)* Alfred, you are coming home!

The courtroom in Rennes. The Guard of 'Dishonour' arrives. They turn their backs to Dreyfus as he is marched into court. As he enters, the spectators break into a gasp. He has become an old, old man of 39. He is pale and strained. He wears the uniform of the artillery. He has difficulty in walking. He stumbles. His uniform flaps around his shrunken body.

Seven judges are present. Large figure of Christ on the wall. Dreyfus salutes the President with his white-gloved hand, takes off his képi and sits. Mercier watches everything, he controls the military. He mounts the witness stand.

MERCIER I swear to speak the truth, nothing but the truth. I hold that the motive for Dreyfus' treason was that he has no feelings of patriotism.

Dreyfus watches Mercier intensely.

MERCIER He was once heard to say when a patriot was lamenting the Alsace-Lorraine: "For us Jews it is not the same, in whatever country we are, our G–d is with us". The treason is clearly evidenced by the prisoner's contradictions and lies and from the technical examination of the 'bordereau'. I have not reached my age without learning that all that is human is fallible. I am an honest man and the son of an honest man. Since the campaign for a re-trial began I have followed closely all the discussions. If the slightest doubt had crossed my mind, I should be the first to declare and to say before Captain Dreyfus: "I have been honestly mistaken"...

Dreyfus electrifies the court. Losing all self-control he hurls himself at Mercier and cries out in a voice of a wounded animal

DREYFUS That is what you ought to say!

Mercier is taken aback and blanches – Dreyfus is forced back into his seat by the guards.

MERCIER I would say, I have been honestly mistaken. I would acknowledge it and do all that is possible to right a terrible mistake.

Dreyfus again in that same unforgettable voice

DREYFUS It is your duty to do so!

MERCIER Well, it is not so. My conviction has not changed since
1894. It has been strengthened by the most thorough study
of the dossier and the utter uselessness of all the efforts to
prove the prisoner's innocence.

JUDGE *(Presiding)* The court will now consider its verdict.

*The judges leave to consider their verdict. There is commotion in
court. Shortly, the judges return. They raise their hands to their
caps in military salute.*

JUDGE *(Presiding)* In the name of the French people. Is Alfred
Dreyfus, Captain in the Artillery, guilty of having dealings
with a foreign power and delivering the documents listed
in the 'bordereau'?

JUDGE I Guilty.

JUDGE II Not guilty.

JUDGE III Guilty.

JUDGE IV *(Presiding)* Not guilty.

JUDGE V Guilty.

JUDGE VI Guilty.

JUDGE VII Guilty.

JUDGE *(Presiding)* The court declares by a majority of five votes
to two that the accused is guilty. Alfred Dreyfus you have
been found guilty... *(his voice is drowned by the crowd)*

*The courtroom begins to empty. Zola, Lucie and Picquart are
stunned.*

LUCIE I feel terror, sacred terror.

PICQUART I feel terror.

ZOLA I feel the sacred terror of rivers flowing back to their
source

LUCIE of the earth turning without a sun.

PICQUART Never has there been a more detestable monument
of human infamy.

LUCIE Human infamy.

ZOLA Even Jesus was condemned but once.

PICQUART Even Jesus.

LUCIE Jesus even.

*The Dreyfusards have gathered near the cell of Dreyfus. Lucie and
Mathieu enter the prison cell area. Mathieu looks at his brother
whose pretended calm hides an inner suffering so atrocious that
Mathieu finds it difficult to control his emotions. Lucie stifles her
tears.*

LUCIE *(To Mathieu)* I am frightened. He wants to see his
    children. Just once more.

MATHIEU *(To Lucie)* We must accept a pardon to save his life.

DREYFUS *(Overhearing, disturbed)* A pardon? That would be
    my final degradation.

LUCIE Your children will grow up fatherless, oppressed by the
    questions they cannot answer. My years alone have drain-
    ed me of life.

DREYFUS My innocence has been my nourishment. The inno-
    cence was my nourishment. My liberty is nothing for me
    without honour. I declare that my innocence is absolute.

LUCIE His innocence is absolute.

DREYFUS Until my dying breath I will fight, fight for its
    recognition.

LUCIE I will fight for its recognition. His innocence is absolute.

DREYFUS My innocence is absolute.

*Demangue returns with an authority for the release of Dreyfus. It
is handed to the prison director. The gates of the cell are opened.
Lucie and Deyfus approach each other and collapse into each
other's arms.*

ZOLA *(From backstage)* The day will come when the truth will
    be understood by all.

*Dreyfus is now quite alone at the back of the stage. He begins to
walk slowly to the front. His walk is interrupted by memories and
associations. Figures, musical themes and sounds from his past
life are seen and heard – the degradation, the Rennes verdict, the
declaration of his innocence, his re-integration into the army.
Finally, the ceremony of the Legion of Honour – the General
touches Dreyfus on his shoulder three times with his sword and
pins the cross on his black dolman. Dreyfus arrives at the front of
the stage. He is old and frail. He salutes the Tricolore. The voice
of Dreyfus as a boy is heard.*

THE BOY DREYFUS Papa, when I grow up I want to be a soldier.

END

Hebrew Prayer *(see p. 77)*

קְהִילָה הַשֵׁם אֶחָד.

CONGREGATION *(Hebrew)* The Lord is One.

חַזָּן א שְׁמַע יִשְׂרָאֵל הַשֵׁם אֱלֹקֵינוּ הַשֵׁם אֶחָד. אֶחָד.

CANTOR I Hear Oh Israel, The Lord our G–d, The Lord is One. One.

חַזָּן ב שְׁמַע יִשְׂרָאֵל הַשֵׁם אֱלֹקֵינוּ הַשֵׁם אֶחָד.

CANTOR II Hear Oh Israel, The Lord our G–d, The Lord is One.

חַזָּן ג שְׁמַע יִשְׂרָאֵל הַשֵׁם אֶחָד.

CANTOR III Hear Oh Israel, The Lord is One.

חַזָּן א אָבִינוּ מַלְכֵּנוּ. כָּתְבֵנוּ בְּסֵפֶר חַיִּים טוֹבִים. אָבִינוּ.

CANTOR I Our Father, Our King, seal us in the book of happy life. Our Father,

אָבִינוּ מַלְכֵּנוּ. בַּטֵּל מַחְשְׁבוֹת שֹׂנְאֵינוּ. אָבִינוּ מַלְכֵּנוּ. אָבִינוּ.

Our Father, Our King, annul the designs of those who hate us. Our Father, Our King, Our Father,

אָבִינוּ מַלְכֵּנוּ. קְרַע רוֹעַ גְּזַר דִּינֵנוּ.

Our Father, Our King, repeal the evil sentence of our judgement.

קְהִילָה (קוֹלוֹת בַּסִּים) שְׁמַע יִשְׂרָאֵל הַשֵׁם אֱלֹקֵינוּ הַשֵׁם אֶחָד.

CONGREGATION *(Bass voices)* Hear Oh Israel. The Lord Our G–d. The Lord is One.

חַזָּן ב / חַזָּן ג אֶחָד.

CANTOR II/III One.

Original *(see pp. 93/94)*	Translation
Polka des Youpins	**The Yid's Polka**

MARIE V'la qu'dans les rues d'Paris
    on n'trouve plus qu'des youdis.
    A chaque pas sur votre chemin
    Vous n'voyez qu'des youpins.
    C'est une race de vermine,
    Ils ont de tristes mines.
    On d'vrait les expulser
    Ou bien les assomer.
MARIE Trala la la la
    lala la la la
    Chassez ces coquins
    Oh! les sales youpins.
CROWD *(refrain)*
MARIE D'après leur reseignements
    Dreyfus est innocent,
    Mais ils sont incapables
    D'découvrir le coupable.
    On peut l'dire sans vergogne
    Ils ont triste besogne,
    Quand leur race périra
    Alors chacun chantera.
MARIE/CROWD *(refrain)*

MARIE Here in the streets of Paris
    Only Yids are to be found
    At each and every turn
    Only Yids are seen around
    Such a race of vermin
    With their pathetic grins
    Should either be thrown out
    Or else be done right in.
MARIE Tra la la la la
    La la la la la
    Kick out the dirty Yids
    Hip! Hip! Hip! Hurrah!
CROWD *(refrain)*
MARIE In their twisted minds
    Dreyfus is not to blame
    Although the guilty party
    Not one of them can name
    Their sordid end is nigh
    So when their race is gone
    We'll celebrate with song
    Holding our heads up high.
MARIE/CROWD *(refrain)*

Original (see p. 97)
Zola ferm' ta boîte

MARIE Quand donc finiras-tu, dis?
      Zola d'défendr' les Youdis:
      Si tu n'veux plus qu'on t'emboîte,
      Ferm' ta boîte!
      Tu n' s'ras pas d' l'Académie
      Maint'nant, c'est bien entendu,
      Finis donc ta comédie:
      T'as assez vendu!
      T'as assez vendu!
CROWD *(Chorus)* Ferm' ta boîte!
      Ferm' ta boîte!
      T'as assez vendu!
MARIE Maint'nant qu' t'es rich' comm' Crésus
      N' viens pas la faire au Jésus:
      Ne prêch' pas d' ta voix benoîte;
      Ferm' ta boîte!
      De l'innocence de ton traître
      Tu restes le seul convaincu;
      Au fond t'en rigol's peut-être;
      T'as assez vendu!
CROWD Ferm' ta boîte! Ferm' ta boîte!
      T'as assez vendu! Assez vendu!

Translation
Zola shut your trap

MARIE When, when, shall we see the end
      of Zola defending his Yid friends?
      If you don't want a kick up the arse
      Shut your trap!
      You'll be out of the Academy
      It is now very clear,
      Finish your comedy
      You've betrayed us quite enough!
      You've betrayed us quite enough!
CROWD *(Chor)* Shut your trap!
      Shut your trap!
      You've betrayed us quite enough!
MARIE Now that you are as rich as Croesus
      Do not put blame on Jesus
      Don't preach in Holy tones
      Shut your trap!
      Of the innocence of your traitor
      You're the only one convinced
      They're probably laughing at you
      You've betrayed us quite enough!
CROWD Shut your trap! Shut your trap!
      You've betrayed us quite enough!

Original (see p. 98)
La Marseillaise Antijuif

CROWD Tremblez, youpins, et vous, perfides,
      Le jour de gloire et arrivé.
      Contre nous de la juiverie
      Le troupeau hurlant s'est levé.
      Le troupeau hurlant s'est levé
      Les voyez-vous dans notre France
      Ces insulteurs de nos soldats,
      Grossis de voyous, de rastas
      Nous narguer de leur insolence.
      Aux armes, antijuifs, formez vos bataillons
      Marchons, marchons
      Qu'un sang impur abreuve nos sillons.

Translation
The anti-Jewish Marseillaise

CROWD Start trembling Yids and traitors
      Despised by one and all
      If the Jews rise up against us
      And avenging hordes will roar
      And avenging hordes will roar.
      Frenchmen it's an outrage
      Our weakness has allowed
      Let's rid ourselves of outlaws
      May Jews be disavowed.
      To arms anti-Semites! Form your battalions!
      March on, march on
      May our fields be drenched with their tainted blood.

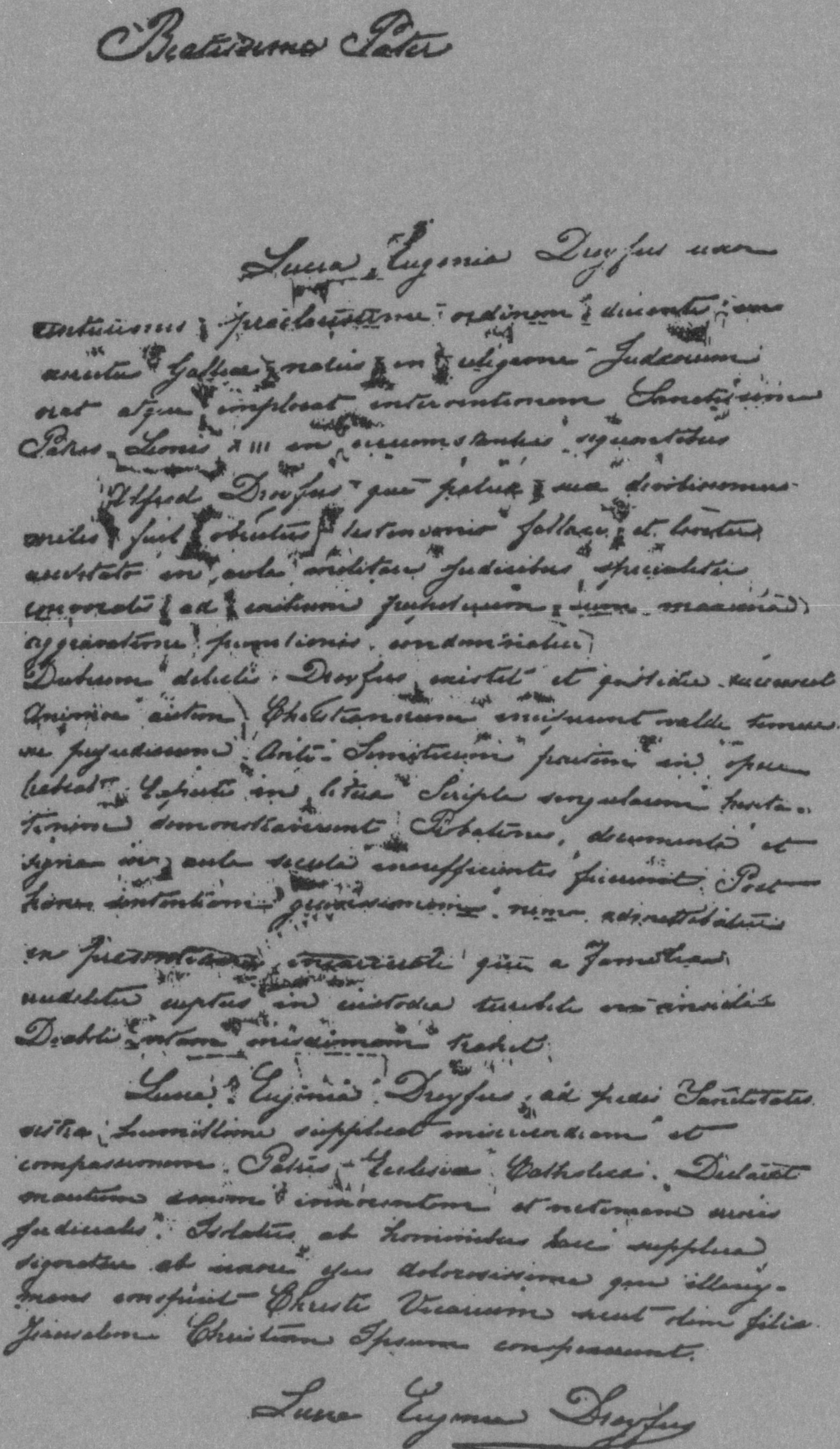

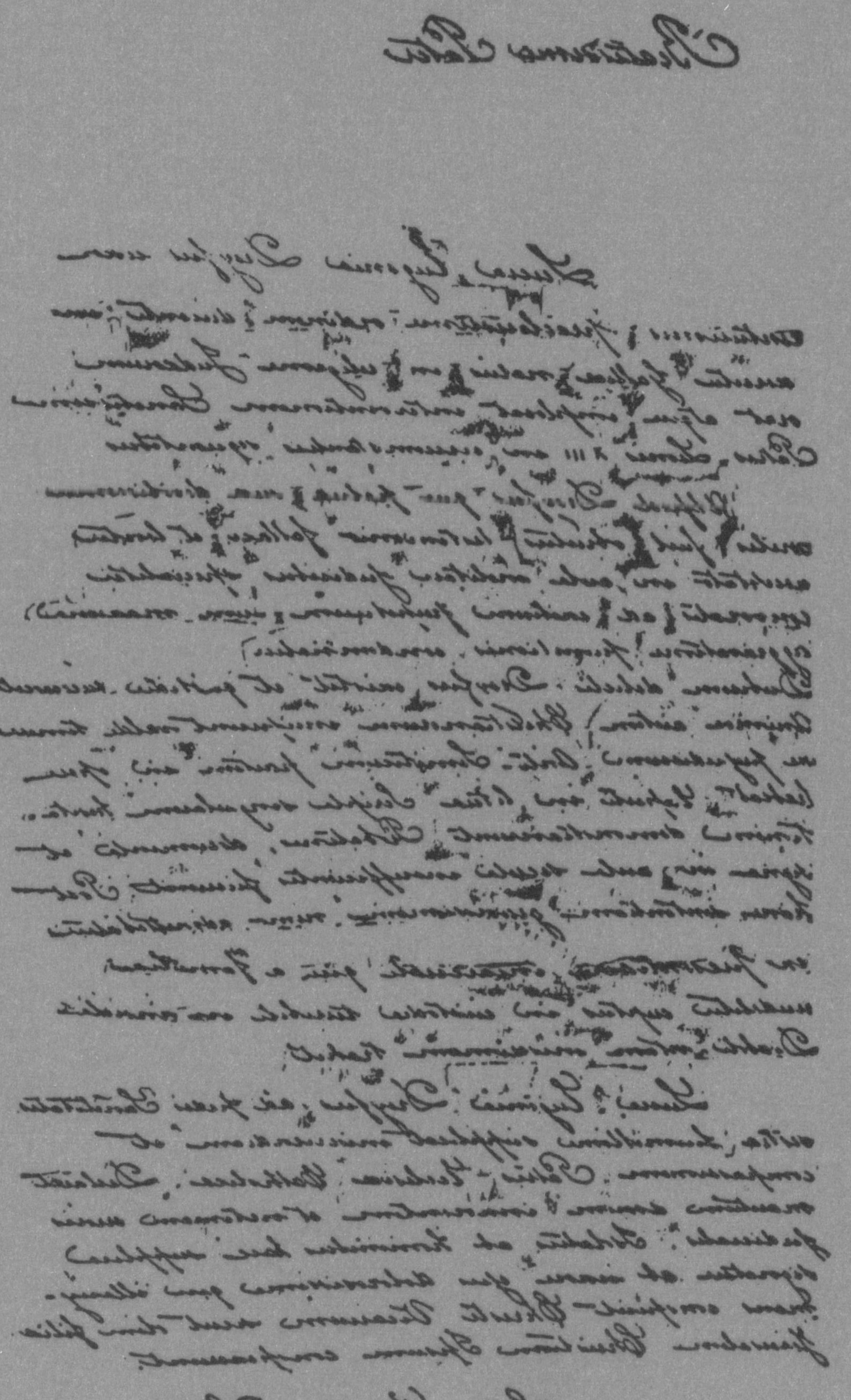

THE SUPPLICATION

Most blessed Father

Lucie Eugénie Dreyfus, wife of a captain holding a brilliant position in the French Army, of Jewish birth, begs and implores the intervention of the Most Holy Father, Leo XIII, under the following circumstances:

Alfred Dreyfus, a soldier most devoted to his country, was tried, before a special court-martial, on evidence both fallacious and frivolous, and condemned by his judges to perpetual exile, accompanied by the severest form of punishment.

A doubt exists as to the crime of Dreyfus, and increases day by day. Moreover, Christian minds are filled with a grave misgiving that anti-Semitic prejudice has had much to do with the matter. Experts in handwriting have shown singular hesitation in forming their decisions. Proofs, documents, and signs alleged before the secret court were insufficient. After the terrible sentence, no one was allowed in the presence of the prisoner who, snatched from the bosom of his family, was conveyed to the Ile du Diable, where he endures a wretched existence.

Lucie Eugénie Dreyfus, prostrate at the feet of your Holiness, most humbly supplicates the mercy and compassion of the Father of the Catholic Church. She declares that her husband is innocent, and the victim of a judicial error. Snatched from all association with humankind as he is, this petition is signed by his grief-stricken wife, who, in tears, looks towards the Vicar of Christ, even as formerly the daughters of Jerusalem turned to Christ Himself.

Sgd. Lucie Eugénie Dreyfus

OPERA, TRUTH AND ETHICS

DREYFUS – DIE AFFÄRE   A MUSICAL TESTIMONY

Alfred Dreyfus at home with his family before his arrest.

Why in Berlin? The question was asked time and again. Was it not a French affair? Do you want to comfort Germans with French anti-Semitism? And then, the most burning question of all, how could you mount this opera in the very city where the destruction of the Jewish people was masterminded? Yet this, for me, was the most compelling reason to stage the opera in Berlin.

Berlin, emphasised Götz Friedrich, did not and would never forget that the greatest atrocities committed against the Jewish people were carried out by the Germans "that is by the Nazis in Germany". The country still had to find a *modus vivendi* with its past "not to forget and not to deny but to come to terms with it". Like Hannah Arendt and George Steiner he felt that the Dreyfus Affair was the seed of a persecution which spread dreadfully. He saw it as an act of solidarity by the Germans with the French that Berlin was the site of the premiere and, in his view, it had a historical claim to be, because from the mid 18th to the mid 19th century, Jewish culture, Jewish language and Jewish religion were not only safeguarded but supported there almost more than anywhere else. But sadly Berlin was also the city from which the orders for mass destruction were given. That was a dreadful fate to live with and for that reason above all the

were their true feelings towards this outsider, a Jew, using their theatre to say "J'Accuse" to the German people? But it was pointed out to me that at no time should I feel an outsider and that it was understood, and even appreciated, that the author, devoted to the subject matter, "wanted to achieve more with this work than just an opera."

Dreyfus: "My sole crime was to be born a Jew."

choice of Berlin for the premiere was so important.

But the questions persisted and their implications grew, creating a veritable prologue to the production. I watched with unease German hands constructing on stage the Star of David, so recently an emblem of death in Germany; I read the anonymous denunciation of the opera and questioned its motives. I was aware of representing the victims and sensed a cautious attitude from those around me. I was uneasy, I was at the crossroads. What

But the ominous clouds of history would not disperse and as soon as the production set sail at the Deutsche Oper in Berlin, the memories of the Holocaust, silent or expressed, became its constant companion. Artistic endeavours were fused with the dictates of history and tested by the demands of conscience. Just as the Dreyfus Affair was a Rorschach test of social morality, *Dreyfus – Die Affäre* became a Rorschach test for its creators, its public and eventually its critics. Could they remain im-

"Our Father, our King. Annul the designs of those who hate us."

Justice resides in the truth alone, concluded Zola at the end of his life in his epic work *La Vérité*. Respect the 'mystique' of the Dreyfus Affair pleaded Charles Péguy in his *Notre Jeunesse*, the ethics of a noble cause inspired by the struggle for justice.

This struggle was waged between powerful social forces which dominated the characters and manipulated the masses. It was these forces which transformed an injustice into an affair; prejudice, racism, nationalism – the constants which are so deeply imbedded into the history of our century. I did not want to rewrite history, I wanted to expose it.

Dreyfus himself was an army man. He was reserved and he was reticent. An 'absent' martyr, he became and remains to this day, a symbol of the fight against injustice. "My sole crime was to be born a Jew" exclaims Dreyfus, the first Jewish deportee. "I am innocent" he declares and speaks universally for all victims of injustice. "Guilty" reverberates the false judgement, "J'Accuse" thunders Zola. "This is the most noble libretto I have ever read" remarked George Tabori "and remember only what is necessary is beautiful". History has passed down to us intact the testimony of this struggle, word by word, phrase by phrase. These constitute the battleground and drama of the Affair and of *Dreyfus – Die Affäre*. Its characters refuse to be fictionalised and demand to speak their historical lines and give their evidence – the truth, the whole truth, and nothing but the truth.

The question was, in the view of Götz Friedrich, whether the opera would have benefited if the author George Whyte had given free rein to invention for the characters and situations or would it have lost by becoming less authentic? The Dreyfus Affair was a special case and there was a

partial when their country was indicted? The past converged with the present.

And, alas, the present underlined the topicality of the opera and how necessary it was, stressed Götz Friedrich, "to work and re-work the guilt of the past". He expressed his concern at the events today, not only in German cities, but in many European countries and not least in Eastern Europe. Racism was not only a national problem but a European problem and wherever racial injustice trod on human dignity and on human rights.

great risk that many people would have objected saying "he is altering history, he is manipulating the facts. In this case, opera as an art form seems to stand at the crossroads as in Oedipus and asks whether historical truth is more important than an artistic truth, however conceived or invented. The Dreyfus opera, and I wish to emphasize this, has brought a new awareness to the debate and this question should, and will, cause intense discussion throughout this opera's wanderings, I hope to many of Europe's stages as well as to those of the United States. I believe that this question concerning truth is and will continue to be ever present."

And the truths met at the premiere. The members of the audience sat absorbed, motionless, submitting to the drama on that inner stage where truth and guilt strive for co-existence. They understood.

So did the critics as title after title was to show: 'The stage as a court of law', 'An important work at the right time', 'Success for anti-racism', 'Opera of the century', 'A work to be experienced', 'Warning for our times' and so on.

They were united on the significance of the opera but divided on its structure and the work ended, as it started, with questions. Did *Dreyfus – Die Affäre* create a landmark by extending operatic boundaries? Was it greater than an opera because of its subject or less than an opera because of its form? Did it transgress or transcend operatic criteria? Was it an operatic Guernica strewn with the dismembered limbs of man's morality? The critics were at the crossroads.

"Whether the title opera is accurate, I cannot decide" remarked Götz Friedrich. Much is included in the term opera. He felt it was rather a protocol as the author had ensured that basically every word sung could be verified historically. Possibly a musical protocol or more exactly a "Protokoll für das Musiktheater". A musical testimony.

Dreyfus – Die Affäre was a success continued Götz Friedrich and joined Berg's *Wozzeck* and

Zola: "Oh the empty accusation! To condemn a man thus."

Margaret Pays The Yid's Polka.

"Lists of Jews for sale".

Janáček's *House of the Dead* which "underlined the humanistic resolve of opera and its permanent, inherent potential to convey a human message. The subject concerns everyone – tua res agitur – it is your business which is being dealt with here. I believe it was a great success as well as necessary and salutory. Especially now, especially today, especially here".

The exposure of truth, in whatever form, is an arduous task requiring unflinching effort and determination. It is fraught with anxiety, disappointments and betrayals. The realisation of *Dreyfus – Die Affäre* took eight years. It became its own Affair.

Why did it take so long? I asked Götz Friedrich. "Sometimes good things have to take their time" he replied.

This article is based on a conversation with Professor Götz Friedrich following the premiere of the opera *Dreyfus – Die Affäre* on 8 May 1994 at the Deutsche Oper Berlin.

DREYFUS

Every man
who is truly a man
must learn to be alone
in the midst of all others
and, if need be,
against all others.

Roman Rolland

DREYFUS EST INNOCENT

LES DÉFENSEURS DU DROIT, DE LA JUSTICE ET DE LA VÉRITÉ

VIVE LA RÉPUBLIQUE

VIVE LA FRANCE!

SCHEURER-KESTNER

EMILE ZOLA

« La Vérité est en marche, rien ne l'arrêtera! »

L. TRARIEUX

GEORGES CLEMENCEAU

YVES GUYOT

JEAN JAURES

Lieutenant-Colonel PICQUART

« Je n'emporterai pas dans la tombe un pareil secret. »

JOSEPH REINACH

Par la Vérité, vers la Justice!

À BAS LES TRAITRES!

VIVE L'ARMÉE!

FRANCIS DE PRESSENSE

FERNAND LABORI

BERNARD LAZARE

SUPPLÉMENT GRATUIT
Au journal " LE SIECLE "

DREYFUS
EST
INNOCENT

LES DÉFENSEURS DU DROIT, DE LA JUSTICE ET DE LA VÉRITÉ

VIVE
LA
FRANCE!

VIVE
LA
RÉPUBLIQUE

L. TRARIEUX

« Derrière l'affaire Dreyfus, ne voyez-vous pas les partis qui s'embusquent? »
Lettre à M. Godefroy Cavaignac

ÉMILE ZOLA

« La Vérité est en marche, rien ne l'arrêtera! »

SCHEURER-KESTNER
SÉNATEUR

YVES GUYOT
ANCIEN DÉPUTÉ, ANCIEN MINISTRE, DIRECTEUR POLITIQUE DU SIÈCLE

« L'honneur de l'armée ne consiste pas à maintenir une condamnation illégale et injuste et à couvrir le coupable »
J. Innocent et Traître

GEORGES CLÉMENCEAU (L'Aurore)
ANCIEN SÉNATEUR

« La France ne serait plus la France si elle retirait de ...»

JOSEPH REINACH
ANCIEN DÉPUTÉ

Par la Vérité, vers la Justice!

Lieutenant-Colonel PICQUART

« Je n'emporterai pas dans la tombe un pareil secret. »

JEAN JAURÈS

VIVE

L'ARMÉE!

A BAS
LES
TRAITRES!

SUPPLÉMENT GRATUIT

Au journal " LE SIÈCLE "

BERNARD LAZARE

FERNAND LABORI, AVOCAT

FRANCIS DE PRESSENSE

SUPPLÉMENT GRAT

Au journal " LE SIÈCLE "

DREYFUS
EST
UN TRAITRE

VIVE LA FRANCE !

VIVE LA RÉPUBLIQUE !

M. CAVAIGNAC

« J'ai la certitude absolue de la culpabilité de Dreyfus ! »

CAVAIGNAC, Ministre de la Guerre.
(7 juillet 1898. — Discours à la Chambre des Députés.)

« Je demeure convaincu de la culpabilité de Dreyfus et aussi résolu que précédemment à combattre la revision du procès. »

CAVAIGNAC, Ministre de la Guerre.
(4 septembre 1898. — Lettre de démission adressée au Président du Conseil, M. Brisson.)

Général MERCIER

« Des notes que j'ai eues en ma possession m'ont été qu'un officier des bureaux de l'État-Major a communiqué à une puissance étrangère des documents dont il avait eu connaissance en vertu de ses fonctions.

« Je l'ai fait arrêter. »

Général MERCIER, Ministre de la Guerre.
(Novembre 1894.)

Général ZURLINDEN

« L'étude approfondie du dossier judiciaire de Dreyfus m'a trop convaincu de sa culpabilité pour que je puisse accepter, comme chef de l'armée, toute autre solution que celle du maintien intégral du jugement. »

Général ZURLINDEN, Ministre de la Guerre.
(17 septembre 1898. — Lettre au Président du Conseil, M. Brisson.)

Général BILLOT

« Dreyfus, en mon âme et conscience de soldat et de chef de l'armée, Dreyfus est coupable ! Dreyfus est un traitre ! »

Général BILLOT, Ministre de la Guerre.
(Décembre 1896. — Déclaration à la Chambre des Députés.)

VIVE L'ARMÉE !

A BAS LES TRAITRES !

En dépôt : 5, rue Saint-Joseph.

DREYFUS EST UN TRAITRE

VIVE LA RÉPUBLIQUE !

VIVE LA FRANCE !

M. CAVAIGNAC

« J'ai la certitude absolue de la culpabilité de Dreyfus! »

CAVAIGNAC, Ministre de la Guerre.
(7 juillet 1898. — Discours à la Chambre des Députés.)

« Je demeure convaincu de la culpabilité de Dreyfus et aussi résolu que précédemment à combattre la revision du procès. »

CAVAIGNAC, Ministre de la Guerre.
(4 septembre 1898. — Lettre de démission adressée au Président du Conseil, M. Brisson.)

Général MERCIER

« Des notes que j'ai eues en ma possession m'ont été qu'un officier des bureaux de l'État-Major ait communiqué à une puissance étrangère des numents dont il avait eu connaissance en vertu de ses fonctions.

« Je l'ai fait arrêter. »

Général MERCIER, Ministre de la Guerre.
(Novembre 1894.)

VIVE L'ARMÉE !

Général ZURLINDEN

« L'étude approfondie du dossier judiciaire de Dreyfus m'a trop convaincu de sa culpabilité pour que je puisse accepter, comme chef de l'armée, toute autre solution que celle du maintien intégral du jugement. »

Général ZURLINDEN, Ministre de la Guerre.
(17 septembre 1898. — Lettre au Président du Conseil, M. Brisson.)

A BAS LES TRAITRES !

Général BILLOT

« Dreyfus, en mon âme et conscience de soldat et de chef de l'armée, Dreyfus est coupable ! Dreyfus est un traître! »

Général BILLOT, Ministre de la Guerre.
(Décembre 1896. — Déclaration à la Chambre des Députés.)

Au dépôt : 3, rue Saint-Joseph.

DREYFUS

*In the world of politics
every action designed
to provide a specific
political response is capable
of generating an equal,
opposite and more than
likely greater,
political reaction.*

Harold Wilson

THE DANCED DRAMA I

... I must go on till the end for my wife and children.

Alfred Dreyfus

In Paris Theodor Herzl had had an experience which convulsed his soul, one of those hours that changes an entire existence ... he witnessed the public degradation of Alfred Dreyfus ... At that moment the thought of the eternal exile of his people entered his breast like the thrust of a dagger.

Stefan Zweig on Theodor Herzl

...we judge a man, condemn him, brand him, dishonour his name forever, that of his wife, that of his children, that of his father, the names of all whom he loves, on the strength of a document that has not been shown to him.

Georges Clemenceau

Anti-Semitism, this imported product from
Germany, will not take root here! No!
France will not disown the emancipation
wrought by the French Revolution! No!
The nation which has been rightly called
the soldier of law and of justice will not
fail in its promise, in its mission.

Hippolyte Prague

Picquart, as a soldier, knew that by maintaining his accusation he was risking everything, his honour, his career, his livelihood and perhaps his life.

Alma Mahler

*... it was then that I began
to question the motives
that rule the human heart.*

Pierre Dreyfus

There is a retribution which sooner or later overtakes every nation that forgets and rejects the eternal distinctions of right and wrong. Neither from the east, nor from the west, nor from the south does greatness come. But G–d is the judge and abaseth the one and exalteth the other.

Hermann Adler,
Chief Rabbi of England,
after the Rennes Trial

DREYFUS J'ACCUSE

THE DANCED DRAMA

PROLOGUE

An eclipse. The sun cannot countenance the injustice on earth.

As a crumpled curtain rises, a large cross with the crucified body of Dreyfus is seen. A black shadow spreads over the image.

ACT I

The Franco-Prussian War 1870

From the Synagogue in Mulhouse, as the religious service is ending, the boy Dreyfus watches anxiously as the German Army marches into his native city. In his distress he runs towards the ark and hesitates between the Torah and the Tricolour. In patriotic reverence, he approaches the flag and swears to become a soldier and drive the enemy from his country.

The successful young officer Dreyfus, the only Jew on the general staff, is on military training on a day of regimental competitions. He wins, but sees the prize awarded to another officer. His spirit is unbroken as he stands isolated in the mistrustful gaze of his fellow officers.

As Dreyfus leaves, the senior officers deliberate with the Minister of War, General Mercier. There has been much espionage with military secrets passing to the enemy. Could it be the Jewish officer? Suspicion leads to conviction and conviction to conspiracy.

Commandant Henry arrives, agitated, with a document recovered from the German Embassy. A spy is at work. He dances his monologue – the Army above all. Bon viveur Major Esterhazy enters – gambler, womaniser, always in debt. Colonel Picquart arrives. In the dance of the 'bordereau' the officers agree that Dreyfus is the spy. But Picquart, unconvinced, withdraws.

The officers proceed to their secret meeting place, the urinals. The plot against Dreyfus thickens. As they exit, Drumont, the anti-Semitic leader walks past with a priest. The officers cross themselves in reverence.

Picquart the thinker, the musician, the intellectual is troubled. He senses a deep conflict within himself. Truth versus the Army. He deliberates in a deeply felt monologue.

In the comfortable bourgeois home of the Dreyfus family, Lucie awaits her husband. She is praying silently. As he arrives – a modern assimilated Jew – she quickly hides the prayer book. He is fulfilled by his life and prospects in the French Army. Lucie and Dreyfus dance a duet. The children burst into the room with Mathieu his brother, and an intimate interlude shows the closeness of the family. It is violently interrupted by loud knocking on the door as two military policeman burst into the room and hand Dreyfus a summons from headquarters.

Dreyfus is examined in the presence of the officers. He is given a handwriting test and accused of espionage. He is handed a pistol to do his duty. Alone, in a dance of incomprehension, he rejects suicide and decides to fight to prove his innocence. He is arrested and Henry escorts him to prison.

As Dreyfus is led to prison, Esterhazy is seen with Schwartz-koppen, the German Military Attaché. Documents and money change hands. Esterhazy, enriched, joins his mistress, the prostitute Marie, to celebrate. In an erotic frenzy the two lovers dance in ecstasy joined by Schwartzkoppen and his partner. They ridicule the French flag in a lewd pas de quatre. Dreyfus tries to clutch it but, as seven judges find him guilty, he slips from the flag and falls.

Dreyfus in his bare prison cell loses his self-control. He is innocent. He hurls himself against the wall. Out of his mind, his face covered with blood, he stands against the crucifix on the wall. The wise and experienced prison director Forzinetti, alarmed, enters the cell to calm Dreyfus and in their duet recognizes that Dreyfus is innocent. Simultaneously, Lucie, on a lower stage, dances a monologue of despair and is later joined by Mathieu who tries to lift her to reach Dreyfus, but she cannot. As the stages converge, they run to each other with the children but a military escort blocks their path as they take Dreyfus to his public degradation. The priest appears again, and Lucie in desperation supplicates the Church for help but to no avail.

In front of a hysterical mob, Dreyfus is degraded, his insignia removed, his sword broken. As he is marched out and put into irons, the army of the anti-Semitic agitator Guérin begins to form. Dreyfus, banished to Devil's Island for life, sees as his parting image, his own effigy burnt by the Guérin Army as it begins its march of hatred, rampage and destruction in a first Kristallnacht heralding the future.

THE DREYFUS CABARET

A Belle Epoque spectacle with dancers, singers and spectators.
Small orchestra on stage.

The Dreyfus 'hits' of the period are sung, danced and performed.
Many famous characters of the period are there. Toulouse
Lautrec, Sarah Bernhardt, Oscar Wilde and others. Numbers
from many countries are performed, reflecting the times and
attitudes to the Dreyfus Affair. Dreyfus is seen on a different part
of the stage, chained and alone, as he dances a solo of anguish.

   Aristide Bruant and Marie are the masters of ceremony. The
characters in the danced drama arrive. Zola now enters and at
first sits quietly amongst the spectators. Drumont arrives and the
Guérin Army marches in. They order Marie to perform racist
numbers and songs of hate. Zola loses control but cannot get his
"J'Accuse" heard as it is swamped in an anti-Dreyfus pan-
demonium. The Cabaret becomes wild as the whole scene
descends into the pit.

ACT II

Zola dances his monologue on justice. Truth is on the march and the truth must prevail. The fight for a retrial is won.

Dreyfus returns from Devil's Island for his second trial. At dawn, in fog, he is marched through the corridor of a guard of dishonour into a courtroom packed to bursting point with army, clergy, press and society. They watch mesmerized as Dreyfus, now an old, old man of 39, tries to march proudly to the witness stand. He falters, his uniform flaps about his emaciated body. He collapses into a chair. He is ill. Underneath a large Cross sit the seven judges.

During the violent trial all the witnesses give evidence. There are constant conflicts. Zola declaims. Picquart is prominent and duels with Henry. The generals act in concert. Dreyfus is delirious and in a coma but suddenly electrifies the court as he hurls himself at General Mercier when he begins to give evidence. Labori, the lawyer of Dreyfus, traps Henry into admitting his forgeries. He is surrounded by a group of army officers and, as they disperse, Henry lies dead in the courtroom. Esterhazy, terrified escapes. Labori is shot. Picquart again fights for the truth.

The seven judges stand, five declare Dreyfus guilty and two innocent. Dreyfus is shattered. He does not understand. He dances a monologue recalling his happier times.

As the court clears the two dissenting judges stay and move towards Dreyfus with Lucie and their friends. They tender to him and slowly, as the years pass, Dreyfus is rehabilitated and awarded the Legion of Honour.

The courtroom fades as Dreyfus dances a duet of exoneration with Lucie but he no longer has the strength. Zola slowly fades away and dies. As his funeral procession passes in the distance, Dreyfus approaches his coffin and is shot. He falls. Lucie moves to protect him and he continues to dance, wounded, supported by her. The procession continues to centre stage and depicts the passing of time. Drumont arrives and directs the followers to turn, exposing yellow stars on their backs. Lucie and Dreyfus watch. She clutches a young child. As the procession recedes it is suddenly interrupted by the music from a contemporary disco bar, which is seen rising on the front stage.

EPILOGUE

One hundred years later.

Dancing and drinking – the time is now and the scene a disco. A local girl dances closely with a foreigner. Trouble erupts followed by fighting. A rousing march begins, the participants are beautiful and young as a new world is being built, but the march turns to hate, violence, destruction, death and apocalypse.

Lucie is alone on stage, a young infant in her arms. The child is terrified of the audience. Lucie stretches out her arms pleading for his future as the curtain closes.

END

ASPECTS OF THE STAGE TECHNIQUE

The stage technique employed for the danced drama enabled the spectator to experience different levels of reality simultaneously.

A large mirror (1) designed by Josef Svoboda, measuring 8 by 4 metres, with a reflective and refractive surface, was hung from the flies. As a screen, archival images were projected on it and as a mirror, the action on stage was reflected in it, permitting a total vision of the choreography and the dancers movements. Historical perspectives were thus intertwined with stage action creating a multi-layered reality.

To achieve the maximum dramatic effects, the angle and height of the mirror could be varied by the use of three winches (2).

Additionally, a curtain was hung on stage in the form of a horseshoe, consisting of a firm but flexible mesh in ribbons of 75 cms width. This enabled free access for the entry and exit of dancers and an open stage floor permitting spectacular crowd scenes and dramatic solo monologues. The material of the curtain could also be utilised as a reflective surface for the projection of historical images.

With this technique, historical and stage drama combined to provide an enhanced reality in which memory was visualised and became part of the staged experience.

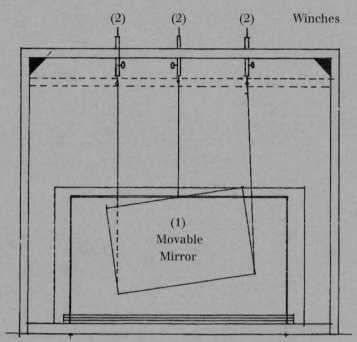

The stage: Frontal View

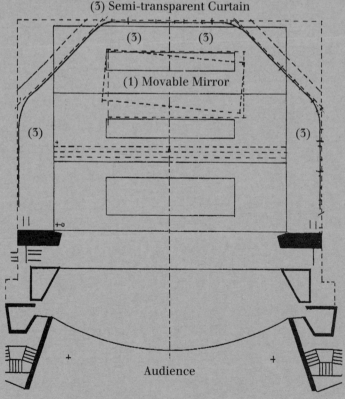

The stage: View from above

THE DANCED DRAMA II

The Dreyfus Affair ... is the culmination of the anti-Semitism which grew out of the special conditions of the nation state. Its violent form foreshadowed future developments, so that the main actors of the Affair sometimes seemed to be staging a huge dress rehearsal for a performance that had to be put off for more than three decades.

Hannah Arendt

We have built imperishable cathedrals on sand.

Sin is whatever obscures the soul.

André Gide

*For I have at last learnt the lesson
that has been forced upon me during
this year, and I shall not ever forget
it. It is that I am not a German, not
an European, but that I am a Jew.*

Arnold Schoenberg

THE OPERA

*If you once condemn a man without the
forms of justice, some day the forms of
justice will be repudiated by others to
harm you.*

Georges Clemenceau

*The Dreyfus Affair has become a
religion, the religion of justice.
Millions of men have felt their
hearts pound for an unknown.*

Bjørnstjerne Bjørnson

*It was the bitterest day
in modern France,
more disastrous
than Waterloo,
more humiliating
than Sedan.*

Hermann Adler,
Chief Rabbi of England,
after the Rennes Trial

*Only truth can stand
up to injustice.
The truth ... or love.*

Albert Camus

*... the innocent always suffer, Monsieur
le Commandant; it is their metier.
Besides, we are all innocent until we
are found out. It is a poor, common
part to play and within the compass
of the meanest. The interesting thing
surely is to be guilty and wear as a
halo the seduction of sin ...*

Oscar Wilde to Esterhazy

*I consider that the worst treason,
perhaps because it is the most common,
is treason to the French spirit, that spirit
of tolerance and justice which has made
us beloved by the people of the earth.*

Georges Clemenceau

*We have watched with indignation
and regret the trial of Captain Dreyfus.
It was less Dreyfus on trial than those
who tried him.*

Governor Theodor Roosevelt

*Even if G–d had
proclaimed from Mount
Sinai that Dreyfus
was innocent one would
not have believed
him in a France made
fanatic by the priests,
the chauvinistic press
and anti-Semitism.*

Eugène Naville

As a consequence of their long social rejection Jews often have a pathological need for honour and... a Jew who has embarked on a career of honour as a General Staff Officer could not commit such a crime... The miscarriage of justice embodied the wish of the enormous majority in France to damn a Jew, and in this one Jew, all Jews... The edict of the great revolution had been revoked.

Theodor Herzl
on Alfred Dreyfus

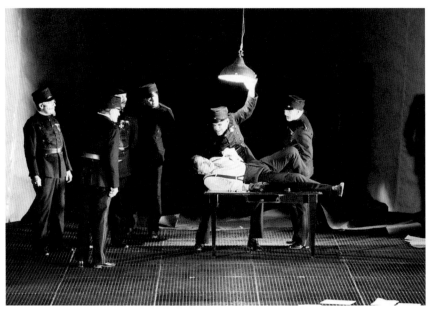

*... how sad it is, however,
that the government of a
great country has resigned
itself ... to be merciful, when
it could have been just ...*

Emile Zola

*A good marriage is
that in which each
appoints the other
guardian of his
solitude.*

Rainer Maria Rilke

*... and we have been left upon them,
without friend or companion, like two
flowers in the wasteland, like two who
are lost, forever seeking something lost
in a foreign land.*

Chaim Nahman Bialik

The greatness of man is his decision to be stronger than his situation.

Albert Camus

*The history of the Dreyfus Affair is dedicated
to all those who burn with righteous
indignation against all forms of injustice,
who open their compassionate hearts to the
innocent and who consider it their supreme
moral duty to right the wrong which has
been committed, who are inspired by the
desire to see the world become richer in love
and humanity, in justice and kindness.*

Bruno Weil

One can get anything one wants from the people when one knows how to rouse them against the Jews.

Roger Martin du Gard

ADMISSION IS NOT ACCEPTANCE II

THE PRICE OF ILLUSION

Dreyfus recalls in his diary how, as a young boy, he cried with sadness as he watched the German Army march into his hometown Mulhouse during the Franco-Prussian War. He swore to become a soldier and drive the enemy from his country. No longer burdened with the name of Abraham or Israel, like his orthodox forefathers who arrived from Rixheim to the land of human rights a century earlier, Alfred kept his promise and began the long march of an assimilationist Jew to become a successful French officer, trespassing the threshold of tolerance in a bigoted terrain which was to lead him to his calvary as a Jew.

But life still smiled on Alfred Dreyfus in 1894. He had married Lucie Hadamard who bore him two children. At the age of 35, he was a captain in the French Army and the first Jew on the General Staff. He did not or would not recognise that admission was not acceptance and thereby became an accomplice to his own martyrdom, forestalling the fate of many others fifty years later who also felt secure in their national aspirations of being German, French or Hungarian.

How often did Dreyfus experience expressions of anti-Semitism and how often did he ignore its warning in the Jew's desperate attempt to be accepted as an equal? What was the mechanism which blinded his yearning and ambition to the dangers around him? Did he not read Drumont's rantings in his *La France Juive* which perpetuated the calumnies which had been levelled at the Jews since the dawn of Christianity? Was he not aware of the editorials in *La Libre Parole* warning against the admission of Jews into the army? Did he really not realise that he was living in a society in which anti-Semitism had become part of its fabric? Did he think he was immune from the longest libel in history?

Dreyfus tried to ignore these impediments and paid for his illusions with degradation, imprisonment and exile. Silent, whispered or spoken he was branded with the same indelible *J* as his forefathers before him and the generations to follow. And, although, in a unique moment of history the injustice to one Jew became a world affair, its lessons were to remain, and still remain unlearned.

History and the passage of time have made the Dreyfus Affair a Rorschach test for all those who come into contact with it. It exposes with troubling clarity bigotry, hypocrisy and guilt. However, a decade of intensive research sadly indicates that little has changed since the Affair erupted. France is reluctant to expose its past, leaving it with a moral limp which cripples the image of a great nation, as it did during the Affair. Germany is the hope and dread of Europe, where a caring youth is tortured by memories of the past being gradually laundered by the tide of nationalism and European aspirations. Fascism winks in the Italian sunshine. Austria flirts with a new leader. Antwerp welcomes the far right. An expanding chain links racists from London to Toronto and Copenhagen to Sydney.

Church dogma and bigoty still imprison true Christian values, stifling an answer to Jeanne d'Arc's simple question "Why don't good Christians make Christendom good?". Prejudice, racism and intolerance remain with their powerful roots unweakened by the tragedies of our century. Fragmented Yugoslavia bleeds from the internal haemorrhage of ethnic cleansing.

And the Jews, are they safe or is their martyrdom to continue? Convinced that it cannot happen again Diaspora Jews prefer to be complacent and impervious to the rumbling terrain around them. Young Israel refuses to see that anti-Zionism is the refashioned cloak of anti-Semitism, harbouring all its traditional dangers. Drancy is desecrated and anti-Semitic acts increase each year. The vision of Edouard Drumont, so valid 100 years ago, begins to haunt many. "The Jews have to be enternally blind as they have always been not to realise what is is awaiting them. They will be taken away as scrap." And he talks with chilling accuracy of the great leader who will suddenly emerge with the "power of life and death and who will achieve a result which will resound throughout the universe. Who is to say that he is not already at work?"

Who is to say?

The grave of Alfred Dreyfus at the Montparnasse Cemetery in Paris was desecrated in 1988.

AUTHOR'S CONCLUSION

Transport No. 62 left Drancy on 20 November 1943. Its destination Auschwitz. In an act of utter degradation, the cargo manifest lists 300 kilos of margarine, 330 kilos of dried vegetables, 600 kilos of canned vegetables and 1118 Jews. Amongst them was Madeleine the grandchild of Alfred and Lucie Dreyfus. She was never to return. The signpost to this tragedy was engraved throughout the centuries and unveiled at the time of the Dreyfus Affair.

No to force, no to injustice, no to tyranny, is the lesson of the Affair, says Jean-Louis Lévy, the grandson of Alfred Dreyfus and the brother of Madeleine and he recounts the story of the explorer who was caught in the polar ice at the time of the Dreyfus Affair. On being rescued, his first question was: Is Dreyfus free? That is the eternal question. Therein lies the eternal struggle.

An injustice becomes an Affair when social passions and conflicting ideologies are aroused. This was the case with the Dreyfus Affair and this was the case with the realisation of its Trilogy.

As soon as work began, resistance to the deeper message of the Trilogy begun to be felt. From animosity to obstruction, from betrayal to physical assault, the disappointments and shocks would have been fatal but for the obsession which became their counter-current. Nor was the media reluctant to abuse its freedom of censorship, while others, with their illusions and prejudices threatened, became and remained antagonists.

But there were allies. Götz Friedrich, a firm but courageous task master; Barthold C. Witte, a steadfast and loyal supporter; Dieter W. Benecke, a staunch and reliable patron and many others who bristle at any sign of injustice. To them all, I offer my gratitude. To those close to me, who suffered the strain and anxieties, I give my love.

To the silent voices of unlived lives, I pledge my undying loyalty as they proclaim endlessly – beware it can happen again.

George R. Whyte
1 March 1996

———

*Injustice anywhere
is a threat to
justice everywhere.*

Martin Luther King

NOTES AND HISTORICAL DATA

J'ACCUSE, history's most famous rallying call to the cause of justice, was written by Emile Zola and published by Georges Clemenceau in *L'Aurore* on 30 January 1898. Over 200 000 copies were sold and it was the watershed that altered the course of the Affair.

THE ACCUSED. This book focuses on the Dreyfus Affair and its deeper implications. In the author's view the Affair is linked through the Jewish fate to essentially three countries: France where it occurred, Germany where the worst excesses of anti-Semitism were executed and the State of Israel which was Herzl's response to anti-Semitism after he had witnessed the degradation of Dreyfus. The focus of this book in no way detracts from the author's abhorrence of all forms of persecution and his deep sympathy for their victims.

PAGE 8 Tua res agitur: "I am specially grateful to you for sending me the page proofs of Wilhelm's Herzog *Dreyfus Case*. I am reading the book – have almost finished it already – with a degree of violent emotion it would scarcely have aroused in me in my unpolitical middle-class German youth. In this very respect I think I am representative of millions of Germans who have travelled the same path and who, like me, will be profoundly stirred as they read by the feeling of Tua res agitur. By Tua res I mean: this is also the cause of your nation, your country, your own conscience. You remark that the author shows present conditions in Germany symbolically reflected in the Dreyfus drama. But that is almost going too far. A stylizing jog to the reader's mind is scarcely necessary or effective. The eternal symbolism, the universal validity, is contained in the powerful story itself; it need only be told – told as powerfully and with such deep feeling as Herzl tells it. Certain passages, in fact whole paragraphs, from Zola's polemics have merely to be quoted to sound staggeringly topical." *From Thomas Mann's letter to Paul Szolnay in 1933.*

Hannah Arendt *The Origins of Totalitarianism*. See bibliography.

PAGE 11 The German Dreyfus Committee: Rainer Barzel, Ignatz Bubis, Ernst-Otto Czempiel, Horst Dahlhaus, Claus-Helmut Drese, Götz Friedrich, Hans-Dietrich Genscher, Hermann Lübbe, Hans Maier, Gian-Carlo del Monaco, Annemarie Renger, Trutz Rendtorff, Ulrich Roloff-Momin, Julius Schoeps, George R. Whyte, Barthold C. Witte.

PAGE 14 The drawing by Henri-Gabriel Ibels, *Dreyfus crucified*, was first illustrated in *Le Figaro* after the Rennes trial in 1899 entitled *Le coup de l'éponge*. The military figure is General Mercier and the reference is from Mathew 27:48: "And straight away one of them ran and took a sponge and filled it with vinegar and put it on a reed and gave him to drink."

PAGE 15 "Justice resides in truth alone and there is no happiness without justice". From Emile Zola's *La Verité* published by Fasquelle 1903.

PAGE 18 Lucie Dreyfus. "Nowhere outside the pages of ancient story can be found an example of womanly devotion and sacrifice surpassing in tragic nobility the example of this French wife and mother." *The Humanitarian, London Mme Alfred Dreyfus, a character sketch, January 1899.*

Emile Zola was found dead in his bed on the morning of 29 September 1902 having been suffocated by fumes from his fireplace. It has been suggested that the chimney had been deliberately blocked.

Dreyfus attended the service at the Pantheon where an attempt was made on his life by Louis Grégori, a military journalist for the newspaper *Le Gaulois* and a member of l'Action Française, the right wing nationalist organisation. Dreyfus was slightly wounded but Grégori was acquitted at the court hearing.

From the funeral oration by Anatole France on the occasion of the transfer of Emile Zola's ashes to the Pantheon in 1908: "Zola discovered not merely a miscarriage of justice. He exposed the conspiracy of all the forces of violence and suppression that had joined hands to kill social justice, the idea of the Republic and the free spirit of France. His bold words awoke France from her sleep. The consequences of his act are incalculable. ... A new order of things originated in his words, based on a fuller justice and a deeper insight into the rights of all ... Do not pity him for what he had to endure and suffer. Envy him! ... Fate and his courage swept him to the summit; to be, for one moment, the conscience of mankind."

The leading figure of l'Action Française was Charles Maurras who later became prominent among Vichy collaborators. He was tried and convicted in 1946. On hearing the verdict he remarked: "The revenge of Dreyfus."

PAGE 19 Picquart who was a fine pianist and musician became a friend of Gustav Mahler and founded the Gustav Mahler Society in Paris. He received news of his appointment as Minister of War during a performance of *Tristan and Isolde* in Vienna conducted by Mahler.

PAGE 20 Henry was found dead in his prison cell with his throat slit by a cut-throat razor. It has been questioned how a prisoner, against regulations, could have had this instrument in his possession. Furthermore, the razor was found in the left hand of the dead man whereas he was right-handed. This fact has raised questions as to whether his death was suicide or murder.

Jules Guérin's headquarters in the Rue Chabrol became known as "Fort Chabrol". It also housed the offices of *L'Antijuif*, a publication representing the Anti-Semitic League.

Schwartzkoppen on his death bed after suffering wounds sustained in the first World War, cried out: "Frenchmen, listen to me! Dreyfus is innocent! He has never done anything. All were forgeries and lies. Dreyfus is innocent!"

PAGE 21 During the Vichy régime the son of Du Paty du Clam, born the day after the degradation of Dreyfus, was appointed "Commissaire aux questions juifs" (head of Department of Jewish Affairs) succeeding Darquier de Pellepoix.

PAGE 22 Between the 3rd and 20th centuries Jews suffered expulsions from and massacres in virtually every country in Europe. "Thus were the Jews burnt at Strasbourg, and in the same year in all the cities of the Rhine whether Free Cities or Imperial Cities or cities belonging to the lords. In some towns they burnt the Jews after a trial, in others without a trial. In some cities the Jews themselves set fire to their houses and cremated themselves. It was decided in Strasbourg that no Jew should enter the city for 100 years but... the Jews (were allowed to come) back to Strasbourg in the year 1368 after the birth of our Lord." *Jacob R. Marcus, The Jew in the Medieval World. Atheneum, New York 1969.*

Page 23 *Le Petit Journal* was an anti-Semitic and anti-Dreyfusard publication and reveals "distortions of journalistic truths and the depth to which antisemitic stereotypes were entrenched. The prominent hooked nose and fleshy lips he (Dreyfus) has been assigned contradict photographic portraits of Dreyfus with his light hair, small nose and clear eyes." *Exhibition Catalogue 'J'Accuse', Norman Kleeblatt.*

PAGE 24 "Theodor Herzl was an assimilated Jew of Hungarian origin who, witnessing the degradation of Dreyfus with its outburst of anti-Semitism, concluded that the only solution to the Jewish question was a national homeland for the Jews. The publication of *Judenstaat* was followed by the first Zionist Congress in April 1897 in Basle, the original venue in Munich having been rejected by the city's Jewish community. In Paris Theodor Herzl had had an experience which convulsed his soul, one of those hours that change an entire existence. As a newspaper correspondent he witnessed the public degradation of Alfred Dreyfus, saw them tear the epaulettes from the palid man while he cried aloud "I am innocent". At that moment he knew in the depths of his heart that Dreyfus was innocent and that he had brought the horrible suspicion of treason on himself merely by being a Jew... at that moment of Dreyfus' degradation the thought of the eternal exile of his people entered his breast like the thrust of a dagger... If humiliation is to be our constant fate, then let us face it with pride. If we suffer because of our homelessness, then let us build our own homeland!" *Stefan Zweig, The World of Yesterday, Viking Press Inc. 1943.*

PAGE 26 Alphonse Bertillon was a handwriting expert called in after the opinion given by Gobert, an earlier expert, proved unsatisfactory.

Carpentras was the first place of refuge for Dreyfus after his release from Rennes. The city was also the site of the worst desecration of Jewish graves in France and took place in 1990.

Dreyfus issued the following statement drafted by Jaurès after his pardon: "The government of the Republic grants me my freedom. It means nothing to me without my honour. Beginning today, I shall persist in working towards a reparation of the frightful judicial error whose victim I continue to be. I want all France to know through a definitive judgement that I am innocent. My heart will only be at rest when there is not a single Frenchmen who imputes to me the crime committed by another." *From Jean-Denis Bredin, "The Affair", Sidgwick & Jackson, 1987 (translated from the French by Jeffrey Mehlman).*

The Protocols of the Elders of Zion were written in France during the Dreyfus Affair (in the view of some, by agents of the Russian secret service) and first appeared in Russia in 1902. It purports to describe Jewish plans for world domination. It is a forgery and was legally declared as such in court proceedings in Switzerland. This anti-Semitic tract has been, and continues to be published and circulated in numerous countries, most recently Poland, Japan and Russia.

Jean Jaurès was a socialist leader, and a member of the Chambre de Députés. Born in 1859, he was assassinated by a member of the Action Française on the eve of World War I.

PAGE 27 The performances at the Théâtre de L'Ambigu in Paris were interrupted by the right wing organisations Camelots du Roi and l'Action Française. The public disturbance and the number of wounded led to the closure of the play by the police.

The Nuremberg Laws were decreed at a Nazi party rally 15 September 1935 disenfranchising the Jews of Germany.

Nazis set fire to 191 Synagogues in Germany and Austria, and ransacked Jewish property and shops. 91 Jews were killed and 30 000 arrested and sent to concentration camps. A fine of 1 billion marks was imposed on German Jewry to cover the costs of rebuilding.

The Vichy Regime enacted increasingly severe measures against the Jews. Large numbers of Jews were rounded up and most of them transferred to the Drancy concentration camp outside Paris for transport to Auschwitz. 75 721 Jews were deported of whom only 2 600 returned.

At the Wannsee conference, in the suburbs of Berlin, on 20 January 1942, presided by Heydrich and attended by top Nazi officials the "Final Solution" coordinating the measures for the extermination of the Jews was agreed.

Poles murdered 42 Jews in a pogrom at Kielce following allegations of the ritual murder of Christian children.

The Military authorities refused to place the statue of Dreyfus in the courtyard of the Ecole Militaire as intended.

Colonel Paul Gaujac, head of the French Army History Services, was dismissed by Minister François Léotard in February 1994 following an article in *SIRPA Actualités*, the army magazine, which described Dreyfus' innocence as "the thesis generally accepted by historians".

For details and analyses of anti-Semitic acts in Europe see *World Report* published annually by the Institute of Jewish Affairs in London and the American Jewish Committee. Germany gives exact figures each year, referring to the Bundeskriminalamt and the Verfassungsschutz.

For details of the Dreyfus Centenary Commemorations see the *Centenary of the Dreyfus Affair – Bulletin of Events*.

PAGE 29 Bernard Lazare born in Nimes, essayist, poet and thinker, was amongst the first to recognise the innocence of Dreyfus.

PAGE 31 Cities where anti-Jewish riots occured included: Paris, Marseille, Bordeaux, Nantes, Rouen, Lyon, Perpignan, Nancy, Dijon, etc. The riots in Algeria were particularly violent.

PAGE 34 The texts of *The Trilogy* are based entirely on documents, writings and songs of the period.

PAGE 57 See the author's article *L'Affaire en Chansons* in *L'Affaire Dreyfus de A à Z*. Flammarion, 1994.

PAGE 66 G–d. According to Jewish tradition the full name only appears in prayers and the Scriptures.

PAGE 74 The unabridged text of the libretto is given with the author's scenic instructions. These are often varied in production.

PAGE 107 A letter was received by the Jewish community of Berlin from a law firm acting on behalf of an anonymous client describing the opera as having anti-Semitic intent and asking for its withdrawal. The Jewish community, after examining the libretto and a meeting with the author, was satisfied that this allegation was unfounded. There were reasons to believe that the political views and motivations of the anonymous accuser were suspect.

PAGE 108 The Rorschach test is used in psychology to examine the personality and reaction of subjects and consists of a black ink blot of indeterminate shape through the interpretation of which the subject reveals his unconscious attitudes.

PAGE 123 The German Army entered Mulhouse on 16 September 1870.

The Barmitzvah which takes place at the age of 13 marks the transition to adulthood of the Jewish male. The Dreyfus family and most of their descendants observed this practice.

The urinals at the Parc Monceau were a favourite rendez-vous for all manners of dubious meetings.

PAGE 124 Esterhazy paid several visits to Schwartzkoppen at the German Embassy in Paris and usually received the sum of 2000 francs on delivery of documents.

Major Ferdinand Forzinetti, the experienced director of the Cherche-Midi Prison in Paris, became convinced of Dreyfus' innocence from his conduct and informed the army authorities accordingly. It was to him that Dreyfus exclaimed: "My sole crime was to be born a Jew!"

PAGE 125 Sarah Bernhardt, the great Jewish actress, was a staunch Dreyfusard and in contact with Zola. She broke off her relationship with her son Maurice over their differing views on the Affair.

Oscar Wilde took an interest in the Affair and knew Esterhazy. *The Ballad of Reading Gaol* was written during his prison sentence which ran concurrently with that of Dreyfus.

Aristide Bruant, the famous cabaret artist and song writer stood for election in the 11th arrondisement in Paris on an anti-Semitic platform.

PAGE 126 The guard of dishonour consisted of 2 columns of soldiers, with their backs turned to the prisoner between them.

Henry insulted Picquart during the Zola trial after which Picquart moved to slap him. The incident led to a duel in which Henry was wounded in the arm.

Maître Fernand Labori was the defence lawyer of Dreyfus at the Rennes trial with Maître Edgar Demange who also defended Dreyfus at his first court martial in 1894 and Zola at his trial in 1898. An attempt was made on Labori's life in Rennes during the trial. He was shot and wounded but the perpetrator escaped.

The backdrop reads (in German): "The day will come when the truth will be understood by all." This quote is from the following statement by Picquart: "The day will come when the truth will be understood by all and why public opinion was misled, why the criminals, the true enemies of the country, were left unpunished. Those, who were too dangerous to touch for it would have meant striking against crimes that were too great."

On 7 September 1995 General Jean-Louis Mourrut the new Head of the Historical Section of the Army, addressing the Jewish Consistory of France at the Hôtel de Ville in Paris and referring to Alfred Dreyfus, declared that "a military conspiracy led to the condemnation and deportation of an innocent".

PAGE 149 The letter *J* was used on German passports during the Third Reich, on the recommendation of Switzerland, to identify Jews trying to enter that country. Paul Grüninger, a Swiss police immigration officer was dismissed in 1939 for ignoring the ban on the entry of Jews into Switzerland and was rehabilitated in 1995, 23 years after his death.

PAGE 152 The French media excised sections which were not complimentary to France. A Bonn newspaper refused to publish readers' letters complaining of an offensive article and the Presserat in Bonn ruled that there were no grounds for complaint. This decision is being contested. Austrian television rejected a documentary film as it did not exhibit 'the right type' of anti-Semitism. Hungarian television excised the libretto from the documentary because it was 'too strong for its public'.

PAGE 161 The bibliography is given in chronological order to enable the reader to gauge the evolution of the Dreyfus literature.

RAGE AND OUTRAGE

Musical Satire in one act
by George R. Whyte

Production
Franco-German
TV Channel La Sept-Arte
and Channel 4 (U.K.)

Orchestration	Luciano Berio
Chanteuse	Ute Lemper
Piano	Jeff Cohen
Orchestra	Ensemble Alternance
Conductor	Diego Masson
Drumont	Lambert Wilson
Zola	Jean-Marc Bory
	(French version)
	George R. Whyte
	(English version)
Director	Raoul Sangla
Painter	Roger Maily
Chorus	Hugues Bataille
	Fabrice Lilamand
	Jean-Jacques David
	Eric Meningand

DREYFUS – J'ACCUSE

Danced Drama in two acts
by George R. Whyte

World premiere
Oper der Bundesstadt Bonn
4 September 1994

Music	Alfred Schnittke
Musical Director	Shuji Okatsu
Choreography	Valery Panov
Stage set and lighting	Josef Svoboda
Costumes	Yolanda Sonnabend
Alfred Dreyfus	Yevgeni Mamrenko
Lucie	Galina Panova
Mathieu	Igor Mikhailov
Picquart	Vadim Bondar
Henry	Alexei Moussatov
Esterhazy	Cyrille de la Barre
Schwartzkoppen	James Anderton
Guérin	Lars van Cauwenbergh
Emile Zola	Didier Gettliffe
Marguerite Pays	N. Hoffmann-Sitnikova
Madame Henry	Larissa Meister
Labori	Dino Baksa
Forzinetti	Andrey Klemm
Rabbi/Priest	Didier Gettliffe
Schwartzkoppen's lady	Nadege Hottier
Schwartzkoppen's friend	Paul Hoffmann
Dreyfus' grandfather	Kajo Meyer
Dreyfus' children	Kathrin Ackermann
	Jörg Schrader
La Goulue	Elizabeth Cooper
Valentin	Paul Hoffmann

Ballet Company of the
Oper der Bundesstadt Bonn

Orchestra of the Beethovenhalle, Bonn

DREYFUS – DIE AFFÄRE

Opera in two acts
by George R. Whyte
Music by Jost Meier

World premiere
Deutsche Oper Berlin
8 May 1994

Premiere at Theater Basel
16 October 1994

Musical Director	Christopher Keene	*Cavaignac, Minister*	Haico Apel
Stage Director	Torsten Fischer	*Ms. Bastian,*	
Stage set and costumes	Andreas Reinhardt	*cleaning lady at the*	
Chorus Master	Karl Kamper	*German Embassy*	Sylvia Müller
Choreography	Darrel Toulon		

Judges. Officers. Soldiers. Populace. Cabaret etc.

Alfred Dreyfus	Paul Frey
Lucie Dreyfus	Aimée Willis
Pierre and Jeanne,	Sören Wynands
their children	Cornelia Wynands
Mathieu Dreyfus,	
his brother	Hagen Henning
Emile Zola	Artur Korn
Colonel Picquart	Barry McDaniel
Major Henry	Peter Gougaloff
Major Esterhazy	Peter Edelmann
Major Du Paty de Clam	Rolf Kühne
Edouard Drumont,	
anti-Semitic leader	David Griffith
General Mercier	Volker Horn
General Boisdeffre	Ivan Sardi
General Gonse	Clemens Bieber
Colonel Schwartzkoppen	Joachim Fischer
Rabbi	Friedrich Molsberger
Cantor I	Kelly Anderson
Cantor II	Peter Edelmann
Cantor III	Klaus Lang
Monk	Josef Becker
General Darras	Jan Herrmann
Prison Director	Günter Gerschler

Chorus of the Deutsche Oper Berlin
Dancers and artists of the Deutsche Oper Berlin

Action takes place in France and on Devil's
Island

*As part of the theatrical events the travelling
exhibition 'J'Accuse' was displayed at the opera
houses of Berlin, Bonn and Basle throughout the
performances. Curator Sarah Nathan-Davis.
Archivist Diane Buckingham.*

BIOGRAPHICAL PROFILES

BERIO, Luciano. Italian. In the forefront of contemporary composers. Studied with Ghedini at Milan Conservatory. Influenced by Dallapiccola and Stockhausen. Central member of Darmstadt circle. Director of Electronic Music Studio in Milan. Collaborated with Italo Calvino and Umberto Eco. Greatly interested in use and development of language in musical performance. Vast output of orchestral, vocal, chamber and operatic works.

FRIEDRICH, Götz. German. General Director of Deutsche Oper Berlin since 1981. Former General Director of the Berliner Theater des Westens. One of the most prominent contemporary stage directors. Studied and worked with Walter Felsenstein and as stage director at the Komische Oper in Berlin. Vast history of works at most major theatres and opera houses throughout the world. Pioneer and supporter of contemporary operatic creations.

FISCHER, Torsten. German. Director of Kölner Schauspielhaus. Established strong reputation through productions in Bremen, Stuttgart, Warsaw, Vienna and Hanover. Numerous awards including Josef-Kainz-Medaille and Karl Skraup-Preis. Has worked on over 45 productions amongst them *Boccacio* and *Perlenfischer* at the Volksoper in Vienna.

GORB, Adam. British. Studied music at Cambridge University under Hugh Wood and Robin Holloway; composition at the Royal Academy of Music in London, graduating with honours. Specialises in vocal and chamber works with particular interest in music theatre. His recently premiered viola concerto received critical and public acclaim.

MEIER, Jost. Swiss. Studied cello, conducting and composition at Bern Conservatory under Rolf Looser and later with Frank Martin. His chamber and symphonic works have been performed throughout Europe, America and Australia. Has gained prominence through his lyrical works which comprise six operas and an oratorio. Professor at Basle and Zurich Music Conservatories.

NATHAN-DAVIS, Sarah. London. International arts feature writer, reviewer and photographer. Member of Association Internationale des Critiques d'Art and Conseil Internationale de la Danse (UNESCO). Contributor to International Encyclopaedia of Ballet and Opera (St. James Press) and Encyclopaedia Judaica. Publishes in national press and cultural reviews worldwide. Photographer with Robert Harding Associates and the Photographer's Libary London.

PANOV, Valery. Israeli of Russian origin. Studied at Leningrad (St. Petersbourg) Academy. Kirov Ballet's outstanding character dancer. Became cause celebre when he applied with his wife Galina Panova to emigrate to Israel. His numerous choreographic works include *Cinderella, The Idiot, The Rite of Spring* (awarded World Critics Prize for best choreography), *War and Peace, The Three Sisters,* etc. Currently ballet director at the Oper der Bundesstadt Bonn.

REINHARDT, Andreas. German. At Berliner Ensemble from 1964 to 1975. Extensive collaboration for operatic and dramatic stage works with Walter Felsenstein, August Everding, Götz Friedrich, Ruth Berghaus and other leading directors. Extensive stage and costume designs worldwide include *Lulu, City of the Dead, Pelleas and Melisande, Oedipus, Katia Kabanova, Intolleranza, Ring of the Nibelungen,* etc.

SCHNITTKE, Alfred. German of Russian origin. Christian and Jewish parentage. Has gained worldwide prominence in recent years. Studied in Vienna and Moscow Conservatories. Influenced by serialism and later by socialist-realist style of Shostakovitch. Adopted Polystylism. Innovative and multi-layered musical textures. Vast musical output includes sixty filmscores. Interested in topical issues. His work *Ritual* commemorates the victims of the Second World War.

SVOBODA, Josef. Czechoslovakian. After practising as an architect he became chief designer for the National Theatre of Prague in 1947 and later its technical director. Has worked in all parts of the world for drama, opera and ballet productions. Collaborated with Sir Laurence Olivier at London's National Theatre. Known for technical innovation. At present artistic director of the 'Laterna Magica' Theatre in Prague.

SONNABEND, Yolanda. British born in Rhodesia. Studied at Academy des Beaux-Arts Geneva and the Slade School of Fine Art London. Specialises in ballet, stage and costume design. Has worked extensively with Kenneth MacMillan at the Royal Opera House, London. An accomplished portraitist. Examples of her stage work are in numerous public collections.

SELECTED BIBLIOGRAPHY

All sections in chronological order

TRIALS AND COURT PROCEEDINGS

Le Procès Zola. Paris. Librairie du Siècle. 2 vols. 1898.

La Révision du procès Dreyfus devant la Cour de Cassation.
   Paris. 4 vols. Stock. 1898/1899.

Le procès Dreyfus devant le Conseil de guerre de Rennes.
   Compte rendu sténographique in extenso.
   Paris. 3 vols. Stock. 1900.

La révision du procès de Rennes 1904/1905.
   Débats de la Cour de cassation.
   Société nouvelle de librairie et d'éditions, 1904.

Enquête de la Chambre criminelle. Paris.
   Ligue des droits de l'Homme. 3 vols. 1908.

Mémoire de M. Henry Mornard.
   Paris. Ligue des droits de l'Homme. 1907.

Décats de la Cour de Cassation. 1906.
   Paris. Ligue des droits de l'Homme. 2 vols. 1906.

HISTORICAL AND LITERARY WORKS

DRUMONT, Edouard. La France Juive. Essai d'histoire contemporaine. Paris. Flammarion 1886.

HERZL, Theodor. Der Judenstaat. Versuch einer modernen
   Lösung der Judenfrage. Leipzig. M. Breitenstein's Verlag.
   1896.

LAZARE, Bernard. Une erreure judiciaire. Paris. Stock. 1897.

DREYFUS, Alfred. Lettres d'un innocent. Paris. P.V. Stock. 1898.

ZOLA, Emile. J'Accuse. L'Aurore Paris, 13 Janvier 1898.

DREYFUS-BILDERBUCH. Karikaturen aller Völker über die
   Dreyfus-Affaire. Berlin. Verlag von Dr. Eysler. 1899.

CONYBEARE, Frederick C. The Dreyfus Case. London. George
   Allen. 1899.

HARDING, William. Dreyfus, the Prisoner of Devil's Island. USA.
   Associated Publishing Company. 1899.

STEVENS, G.W. The Tragedy of Dreyfus. New York. Harper.
   1899.

FRANCE, Anatole. Histoire contemporaine. L'Anneau d'amé-
thyste. Monsieur Berget à Paris. Paris. Calmann-Lévy
1899/1900.

DREYFUS, Alfred. Cinq Années de ma vie. Paris. Fasquelle.
1901. Also published in English and German.

ZOLA, Emile. La vérité en marche. Paris. Fasquelle. 1901.

NILUS, Sergyei. The Protocols of the Elders of Zion. 1902.
A forgery which has been published in most languages.

REINACH, Joseph. Histoire de l'Affaire Dreyfus. 7 vols.
La Revue Blanche et Fasquelle. 1903-1911.

FRANCE, Anatole. L'Ile de Pengouins. Paris. Calmann-Lévy.
1905.

PÉGUY, Charles. Notre Jeunesse. Paris. Gallimard. 1913.

LEBLOIS, Louis. L'Affaire Dreyfus – L'Iniquité La Réparation.
Librairie Aristide Ouillet. Paris. 1929.

SCHWARTZKOPPEN, Count Maximilian von. Die Wahrheit
ueber Dreyfus. Berlin. Verlag für Kulturpolitik, 1930.
Also in French. Also in English.

WEIL, Bruno. Der Prozess des Hauptmanns Dreyfus. Berlin.
Grunewald. Dr. Walter Rothschild. 1930. Also in French.

HERZOG, Wilhelm. Der Kampf einer Republik – Die Affäre
Dreyfus. Büchergilde Gutenberg. Zurich/Vienna/Prague.
1933.

BLUM, Léon. Souvenirs sur l'Affaire. Paris. Gallimard. 1935.

DREYFUS, Pierre. Dreyfus. His Life and Letters. London. Hutt-
chinson & Co. 1937.

SARTRE, Jean-Paul. Réflexions sur la question juive. Paris.
P. Morihieu. 1946.

ARENDT, Hannah. The Origins of Totalitarianism. New York.
World. 1951.

PROUST, Marcel. Jean Santeuil. Paris. Gallimard. 1952.

CHAPMAN, Guy. The Dreyfus Case. London. Rupert Hart-
Davis. 1955.

HALASZ, Nicholas. Captain Dreyfus: History of a Mass Hysteria. New York. Simon and Schuster. 1955.

PALÉOLOGUE, Maurice. Journal de l'Affaire Dreyfus 1894-
1899 (L'Affaire Dreyfus et le Quai d'Orsay). Paris.
Plon 1955.

BOUSSEL, Patrice. L'Affaire Dreyfus et la presse. Paris.
A. Colin. 1960.

THOMAS, Marcel. L'Affaire sans Dreyfus. Paris. Fayard. 1961.

MITTERAND, Henri. Zola Journaliste: de L'Affaire Manet à
L'Affaire Dreyfus. Paris. A. Colin. 1962.

GAUTHIER, Robert. "Dreyfusards!" Souvenirs de Mathieu
Dreyfus et autres inédits. Paris. Collection Archives
Julliard. 1965.

SORLIN, Pierre. La Croix et les juifs (1880-1899). Paris. Grasset. 1967.

MARRUS, Michael R. Les juifs en France l'époque de l'Affaire Dreyfus. Paris. Calmann-Lévy. 1972.

SNYDER, Louis L. The Dreyfus Case. A documentary History. New Jersey. 1973.

PAXTON, Robert O. Vichy France Old Guard and New Order. New York. 1975.

ELBAZ, André. Correspondence d'Edmond Fleg pendant l'Affaire Dreyfus. Paris. A.G. Nizet. 1976.

DREYFUS, Mathieu. L'Affaire telle que je l'ai vécue. Paris. Grasset. 1978.

WILSON, Nelly. Bernard Lazare. New York. Cambridge University Press. 1978.

WILSON, Stephen. Ideology and Experience: Antisemitism in France at the time of the Dreyfus Affair. The Littman Library of Jewish Civilisation. Oxford. 1982.

WINOCK, Michael. Edouard Drumont et Cie. Paris. Le Seuil. 1982.

GROSSER, Paul. E. and Edwin G. HALPERIN. Antisemitism, Causes and Effects. Philosophical Library of New York. 1983.

STERNHELL, Zeev. Ni droite, ni gauche, l'Idéologie fasciste en France. Paris. Le Seuil. 1983.

BREDIN, Jean-Denis. The Affair. Paris. Juillard. 1983. Also published in English.

COSNIER, Colette. Rennes pendant le procès Dreyfus. Paris. Ouest France. 1984.

KLARSFELD, Serge. Vichy – Auschwitz. Paris. Fayard. 1985.

KLEEBLATT, Norman. The Dreyfus Affair, New York. The Jewish Museum. 1987.

DURIN, Jacques. Emile Zola et la question juive. Paris. Edition GM. 1989.

WEBSTER, Paul. Pétain's Crime. London. Papermac. 1990.

WISTRICH, Robert. Anti-Semitism, the Longest Hatred. London. Thames Methuen. 1991.

BURNS, Michael. Dreyfus, a Family Affair 1789-1945. London. Harper Collins, New York. 1991. Also in French.

VIDAL-NAQUET, Pierre. Les Juifs, la Mémoire et le présent. Paris. La Découverte. 1991.

BIRNBAUM, Pierre. La France de l'Affaire Dreyfus. Paris. Gallimard. 1994.

BIRNBAUM, Pierre. L'Affaire Dreyfus – La République en péril. Paris. Découvertes Gallimard 1994.

BASCH, Françoise. Victor Basch ou la passion de la Justice de l'Affaire Dreyfus au crime de la milice. Paris. Plon. 1994.

DROUIN, Michel. L'Affaire Dreyfus de A à Z. Paris. Flammarion. 1994.

DUCLERT, Vincent. L'Affaire Dreyfus. Paris. La Découverte. 1994.

DENIS, Michel, Michel LAGRÉE et Jean-Yves VEILLARD. L'Affaire Dreyfus et l'opinion publique. Rennes. Presses Universitaires des Rennes. 1995.

SCHOEPS, Julius H. Dreyfus und die Folgen. Berlin. Druckhaus Heinrich. 1995.

THEATRE

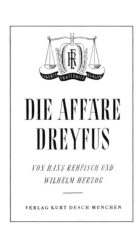

ROLLAND Romain. Les Loups. Morituri. Georges Bellais. 1898.

DU GARD Roger Martin, Jean BAROIS. Paris Revue française. Gallimard. 1913.

REHFISCH, Hans & William HERZOG. Die Affäre Dreyfus. München. Verlag Kurt Desch. 1929.

REHFISCH, Hans & William HERZOG. L'Affaire Dreyfus. Paris. French version by Jacques Richepin. Albin Michel 1931.

EYDOUX, Emmanuel. Capitain Alfred Dreyfus. Marseille. Roger Eisinger. 1967.

ELLIS, A.E. Grand Manoeuvres. London. National Theatre. 1973.

GRUMBERG, Jean Claude. Dreyfus. Serge Oduniec. Paris. Stock. 1974.

LAFONT, Pierre and Claude CONFORTES. J'Accuse. Paris 1995.

QUESEMAND, Anne & Laurent BERMAN. Le Tournage Ensorcele. Paris. Théâtre à Bretelles. Paris. 1995.

MUSICAL WORKS

MAGNARD, Lucien Denis. Hymne à la Justice. For Orchestra. 1903.

DREYFUS. Mordecai Newman and Morris Moshe Cotel. 1985. English/German versions.

THE DREYFUS TRILOGY George R. Whyte. 1994 comprising:
Rage and Outrage. Musical satire. Orchestration Luciano Berio. French/English versions.
Dreyfus – Die Affäre. Opera. Music by Jost Meier. German/English versions.
Dreyfus – J'Accuse. Danced Drama. Music by Alfred Schnittke. Choreography by Valery Panov.

DREYFUS coupable pour l'exemple. Jacques Tchamkerten et Nabli Mili. 1994.

CHANSONS (1898/1899)

VIVE L'ARMÉE, paroles et musique d'Antonin Louis. Édition
Musicale française.

LA FRANCE AUX FRANÇAIS, paroles de Thomas de la Borde,
musique de A. Weiber. Ed. Vve. Hardy.

LA GUEULE À ZOLA Grand duo chanté par Zola et Dreyfus au
casino de l'île du Diable, paroles de Jean François Latrique, sur l'air de 'La berceuse verte'. Ed. Léon Hayard.

ZOLA ÜBER ALLES, paroles d'Emilie Dühring. Musik von
Franz-Joseph Haydn. Berlin. Ed. Moderner Völkergeist.

LE SANS-PATRIE, paroles de Ló Lelièvre, musique d'Émile
Spencer. Ed. A. Repos, Pascals et Uffler.

L'INNOCENCE DE DREYFUS – LE MARTYR DE L'ÎLE DU DIA-
BLE, paroles de J. Jamar et Michel Piéters, musique de
M. Piéters, Liège. Ed. M. Piéters.

COMPLAINTE DU VÉNÉTIEN ZOLA, sur l'air du 'Juif errant'.
Ed. Léon Hayard.

ZOLA FERM' TA BOÎTE! T'AS ASSEZ VENDU!, paroles de Jean
Latrique, sur l'air de 'A Menilmontant'. Ed. Léon Hayard.

J'ACCUSE! LA PREUVE, paroles et musique d'Alfred Grimaldi.
Ed. A. Grimaldi.

L'AFFAIRE, parole de Constant Saclé, musique d'Émile Du-
hem, Vincinnes. Ed. La Gaîté gauloise.

COMPLAINTE DU PRISONNIER, paroles et musique de
K.V. Feldman, Moscou. Ed. Sklade.

HYMNE À LA VÉRITÉ, parols de Clara Delay, musique de Louis
Bost. Lausanne. Ed. Foetisch Frères.

DREYFUSS ZOLA-LIED. Text: Alois Kutschera, nach dem Lied
'Weisst du Mutter was ich träumt hab'. Ed. Wolfgang
Steinitz.

DREYFUS ÜBER ALLES Text: Emilie Dühring, Musik: Franz-
Joseph Haydn. Berlin: Ed. Moderner Völkergeist.

L'INTERROGATOIRE DE DREYFUS – IL N'EST PAS COUPABLE!!!
– IL EST DÉJÀ COUPÉ!!! paroles de A. d'Halbert, sur l'air
de 'La Palmpolaise'. Ed. Léon Hayard.

LA MARCHE ANTISÉMITE paroles de Max Régis, musique de
Cris de guerre. Voie orale.

LA MARSEILLAISE ANTIJUIVE parole de Plume au vent et
Charles de Téméraire, musique de Rouget de Lisle.
Ed. L'Agence antijuive.

LA SÉRÉNADE DU FORT CHABROL paroles de Jules Guérin,
sur l'air d'Au clair de la lune. Ed. Léon Hayard.

À BAS LES JUIFS! – MARCHE DES NATIONALISTES paroles et
musique de Coeur de Franc. Ed. La librairie antisémite.

VOS GUEULES! JUDAS! paroles et musique de Charles Aubert.
Ed. À la Librairie.

LA POLKA DES YOUPINS paroles de Félix Sorlin, sur l'air de
'La Polka des Anglais'. Ed. Léon Hayard.

LA VÉRITÉ EN MARCHE. Bob (Comtesse Sibylle de Janville,
also called Gyp). Le Rire.

FILM AND TELEVISION

Feature films

L'AFFAIRE DREYFUS Georges Mellès. 15'. France. 1899.
(Series of 12 one minute films.)

L'AFFAIRE DREYFUS Zecca and Nonguet. 19'. France. 1907
(Pathé).

DREYFUS Richard Oswald. 1H52', Germany. 1930.
(starring Fritz Kortner).

DREYFUS F.W. Kraemer. 1H29'. Great Britain. 1931 (Directed
by Milton Rosmer, starring Sir Cedric Hardwicke).

THE LIFE OF ÉMILE ZOLA William Dieterle. 1H54'. USA. 1937
(Music by Max Steiner, starring Paul Muni as Zola and
Josef Schildkraut as Dreyfus. Warner Bros. 3 Academy
awards).

I ACCUSE Sam Zimbalist. 1H39'. Great Britain. 1958 (Screen-
play by Gore Vidal, starring Jose Ferrer as Dreyfus and
Anton Walbrook (née Adolph Wohlbruch) as Esterhazy).

L' AFFAIRE DREYFUS Jean Vigne. 16'. France. 1965.

ÉMILE ZOLA OU LA CONSCIENCE HUMAINE Stella Lorenzi. 1978.
1. Un homme assez courageux. 1H56'.
2. J'Accuse. 2H03'.
3. Cannibales. 1H48'.
4. J'Attend toujours. 1H48'.

Television and Video

DREYFUS OU L'INTOLERABLE VÉRITÉ Jean Cherasse. 1H30'.
France. 1975 (Narrated by Jean Claude Brialy).

DREYFUS Hans Schweikart. Germany. 1976.

TROTZDEM Karl Fruchtmann. 2H15'. 1989.

PRISONER OF HONOUR Ron Hutchinson. HBO. USA. 1992
(Directed by Ken Russell, starring Richard Dreyfuss).

RAGE AND OUTRAGE George R. Whyte. 54'. 1994.
French/English versions.

DREYFUS – DIE ODYSSEE DES GEORGE WHYTE 54'. 1995.
German/English/Swedish/Hungarian versions.

DREYFUS – J'ACCUSE George R. Whyte. 1H10'.
German/Swedish versions.

L'AFFAIRE DREYFUS Yves Boisset et Jorge Semprun.
Part 1: 1H20', Part 2: 1H40'. 1995.
French/German versions.

PHOTOGRAPHIC CREDITS AND COPYRIGHTS

The number of the page is given. If necessary, the position is
mentioned by l (left), r (right), t (top), m (middle)
or b (bottom). In case that no position is mentioned all the
material belongs to the named copyright-holder.

Artial Archives
12, 14, 16, 17, 18, 19, 20, 21, 22, 23, 24,
transparencies between 24/25, 26, 27,
30, 31, 57, 58, 59, 60, 61, 62, 63, 66, 69,
70, 71, 77, 105, 115 l, 129 r, 132, 134 l.

Author's Archive
28, 32, 54, 55, 56,
transparencies between 64/65, 65, 87, 88, 89,
transparencies between 89/90, 90, 91,
transparencies between 104/105 and 112/113,
151, 161, 162, 163, 164, 165, 166.

Deutsches Theatermuseum,
Archiv Ilse Buhs/Jürgen Remmler
142, 143, 144 b, 145, 146, 147, 148.

Kranichphoto
106, 107, 108, 109, 110 b, 111, 133 t, 133 b, 135, 136, 139 b.

Jürgen Materna, Ballet der Bundesstadt Bonn 128.

Sarah Nathan-Davis
Author's picture front-flap, cover illustration,
118, 120 b, 131 b.

Stefan Odry
114 r, 119 l, 119 r.

Peter Schnetz
110 t, 134 r, 137, 138 l, 139 t, 144 m.

Stane Sršen
114 l, 120 t, 129 l, 130 l, 130 r, 131 t.

Jennie Walton
115 r, 116, 117 t, 117 b.

AUTHOR'S ACKNOWLEDGEMENTS

George R. Whyte expresses his gratitude to

Dieter W. Benecke; Götz Friedrich; Jean-Louis Lévy; Barthold C. Witte

Luciano Berio; Horst Dahlhaus; Udi Eichler; Eva Foley-Comer; Christopher Keene; Philippe Lévy; Diego Masson; José Montes-Baquer; Sarah Nathan-Davis; Valery Panov

Zvi Ben-Shalom; Jean-Denis Bredin; Diane Buckingham; Michael Burns; Michael Dittmann; Claus-Helmut Drese; Jacques Durin; Yvette Bernard-Farnoux; Isabelle Fessaguet; Adam Gorb; Laurence Harbottle; Norman Kleeblatt; Dorothee Koehler; Anthony Legge; Per Magid; Elizabeth Maxwell; Shimon Samuels; Renate Vollmer; Willy Witty

Diane Afoumado; Ursula Baker; Caroline Whyte-Buchler; Nicky Graca; Vidar Jacobsen; Jeanette Jacubowski; Doris Langer; Livia Parness; Sophie Rosenfeld; Jenny Walton; Wendy Whitworth

François Bellanger; Migros-Genossenschaft-Bund, Direktion Kultur und Soziales, Zürich; Pro Helvetia, Zürich; Ellen Ringler; The Stanley Thomas Johnson Foundation, Berne; Stiftung Deutsche Klassenlotterie, Berlin

Archivio Segreto Vaticano; Leo Baeck Institute, New York; Bibliothèque Cantonale et Universitaire, Lausanne; Bibliothèque Historique de la Ville de Paris; Bibliothèque Municipale de Mulhouse; The Bodleian Library, Oxford; The British Library, London; Zentrale Bibliothek der Freien Universität, Berlin; Centre de Documentation Juive Contemporaine, Paris; Fondation Bellanger, Martigny; Jewish Museum, New York; The Hebrew University, Jerusalem; The Houghton Library, Harvard University, Massachusetts; The Jewish Chronicle Library, London; Kunstbibliothek und Staatsbibliothek der Stiftung Preußischer Kulturbesitz, Berlin; The Knesset Archives, Jerusalem; Musée de Bretagne, Rennes; The Public Library, New York; Österreichische Nationalbibliothek, Wien; Staatsbibliothek, Wien; Zentrum für Antisemitismusforschung, Technische Universität Berlin; The Sourasky Central Library, Tel Aviv; Wiener Library-Institute of Contemporary History, London; Yale University Library, Connecticut

members of the Dreyfus family,
and the many other private and public sources.